When's
God
Gonna
Call Me
BACK?

When's **God** Gonna **Call Me** BACK?

RECONNECTING WITH YOUR CREATOR

Marge Fenelon

Liguori
LIGUORI, MISSOURI

Imprimi Potest: Thomas D. Picton, C.Ss.R.
Provincial, Denver Province
The Redemptorists

Nihil Obstat: Rev. Thomas Knoebel
Censor Librorum, June 7, 2010

Imprimatur: Most Rev. Jerome E. Listecki
Archbishop of Milwaukee, June 23, 2010

Published by Liguori Publications
Liguori, Missouri
To order, call 800-325-9521
www.liguori.org

Library of Congress Cataloging-in-Publication Data
    When's God gonna call me back? / Marge Fenelon.
      p. cm.
    ISBN 978-0-7648-1914-8
    1. Ex-church members—Catholic Church. 2. Catholic Church—Membership.
3. Catholic Church—Apologetic works. I. Title.
    BX2347.8.E82F46 2010
    282.09'0511—dc22
                                                                2010022263

Liguori Publications, a nonprofit corporation, is an apostolate of the Redemptorists. To learn more about the Redemptorists, visit Redemptorists.com.

Printed in the United States of America
14 13 12 11 10   5 4 3 2 1
First edition

To Pitter, thanks for the challenge!

Special thanks to the staff of the Archdiocese of
Milwaukee for their enthusiastic help and support.

Special thanks to the priests in my life who, through their
own human limitations, have taught me to love the Church
even more because of its own. Most especially, my thanks to
the many priests who have been an example of benevolence,
kind fatherliness, and heroic service—Father Dieter in particular.

Contents

Introduction

I was at my nephew's wedding, milling around and catching up with extended family. One of my relatives approached, someone critical of my Catholic faith with whom I'd unsuccessfully debated religion in the past. As long as we talked about inconsequential things like the weather, we were OK. But if the Church came up, it could quickly escalate into full-blown war. I was on guard.

"So, I saw your book," she said, referring to *When's God Gonna Show Up?*, which was published earlier that year.

I froze.

"I didn't read it, but I looked through some of it," she said.

I braced myself for some kind of slam against my faith. I could already feel myself becoming irritated.

"You're a [expletive] good writer," she said.

I was stunned but still suspicious. "Thank you," I muttered, not knowing what else to say.

"My husband says you're a [expletive] good writer, too," she added.

"I'm glad he thinks so," I said, still fishing for words.

"You know, you should write a book like that for people like me." Now I was really stunned. "People like you?"

"Yeah, people like me. You know, lapsed Catholics."

"Lapsed Catholics?"

"If you wrote a book like that for people like me," she said, "I'd come back to the Church."

Truthfully, I was so shocked that I don't even remember how I responded. I might not have responded at all, at least not at that moment. Had she not brought up her proposition again during the course of the evening, I would have thought it was just the wine talking. I assured her that I'd talk to my editor at Liguori Publications and see what I could do. The challenge was on.

You know the rest of the story, of course. You're holding it in your hands right now. While I haven't always been as good as I'd like to be, I've never left the Church. So, if I was going to write a book for lapsed Catholics, I'd have to do some research. *When's God Gonna Call Me Back?* is the culmination of that research.

I sent word through a variety of communication channels, asking three questions:

1. Why did you leave the Church?
2. What kept you away?
3. What brought you back?

Over a period of several months, I received stories from lapsed and episodic Catholics from all over the country—even some from foreign countries—describing their experiences.

I offered them a deal. If they'd be up front and honest with me, I'd withhold all judgment and refrain from any proselytizing. All I wanted to do was listen. I promised them complete confidentiality and the masking of any identifying factors, so that each individual could share without consequence.

It worked. The e-mails, letters, and phone calls poured in. Not only were they frank with me, they were starkly honest in sharing their experiences, confusion, pain, and—in the cases of those who eventually returned to the Church—absolute joy at coming home.

I marveled, cried, fretted, and laughed right along with them. As I opened each e-mail or letter and picked up the phone for each call, I prayed for the person who was about to share with me, asking God's grace and guidance for them and for all they carried in their hearts. I'm still praying for them and will continue to do so.

I'm completely humbled that these individuals trusted me enough to confide some of the most difficult things they've ever said to anyone. I'm proud of them for having had the courage to face their demons, so to speak, and for being brave enough to share their experiences. I'm grateful to them for generously opening up their hearts to others who may suffer from the same or similar circumstances. I know it wasn't easy for them.

I hope you're also grateful to them, because you're the beneficiaries of their strife and wisdom. Whether you're a lapsed or episodic Catholic or the relative or friend of one, you have nothing to lose and everything to gain by reading this book. I'm sure you'll find a bit of yourself or your loved ones in the persons and circumstances described in these pages. Read them. Hear the voices behind them. Relate to them. Reflect on them. Pray about them. Allow yourself to take another look at the Catholic Church, this time through different eyes. I'm sure you'll be pleasantly surprised at what you see.

MARGE FENELON
YEAR FOR PRIESTS

1
Heading
Out

I had to lay down the law early in our marriage. One night, as I wailed and carried on about a situation in which I felt I'd been treated unjustly, my husband tried to console me. In his calm, matter-of-fact way, he said, "Don't be angry."

Bang! I exploded. I railed at him, seething and clenching my fists. "Don't you ever again tell me not to be angry! I can be angry if I want! You have no idea how I feel!" Poor guy. All he was trying to do was comfort his distressed wife.

I, on the other hand, was furious and needed to vent my frustration. It was the first step in trying to figure things out. Being told not to be angry only made me angrier and more frustrated. It made me feel as though nobody cared about how I felt or what had happened to me. Mark did care, but as a brand-new husband he didn't know quite how to get that across to me.

After that, we developed a system in which Mark would graciously allow me to vent, listening carefully, nodding, and stopping me only for clarification. When I had finished venting, he would ask a single question: "Do you want me to do anything about this?" Most of the time I'd decline his offer, but occasionally I'd accept.

The stories in this chapter remind me of that newlywed argument. The people involved have experienced injustice, trauma, heartbreak, and disillusionment. They needed to tell their stories—to vent, so to speak—without having anyone necessarily do anything about it. At times I had to seek clarification, but mostly I just listened. It's the first step in trying to figure things out.

Politics From the Pulpit

Jason hadn't been to Mass in at least three years. The last time he'd gone, he'd been disgruntled by the homily. The priest had been speaking about the secular media and its liberal views. He'd gone to church for Mass, not to hear about the liberal media. He left the church in a huff and couldn't bring himself to go back the next Sunday.

That Sunday turned into many Sundays. His wife was distressed over his refusal to go to Mass and begged him to return. This went on week after week. Deep inside, Jason missed going to church, and he felt badly that he was hurting his wife. So, one Sunday morning, he woke up and decided to give it another try. Perhaps things would be different this time. His wife was ecstatic.

Things weren't different. In fact, from Jason's perspective, they were even worse. This Sunday, the homily was about politics and taking God along into the voting booth. The priest was encouraging the congregation to vote for a prolife candidate and speaking against the culture of death and its threat to society. Jason understood the Church's stance on abortion, but didn't think it should be preached from the pulpit. Additionally, he didn't understand why the Church spoke against abortion but not war. Wasn't the Church concerned about the hundreds of thousands of men, women, and children who died in wars? And what about the death penalty? Why didn't the Church preach to people about voting for candidates who opposed that? Wasn't that a "life issue" as well? And what about protecting the child after birth? None of this made any sense to Jason, but it made him furious.

He and his wife didn't even stay for the rest of Mass. They left, and Jason swore that he'd never go back. He didn't go to church to hear about politics; he went to pray and celebrate Mass. He believed that the Church had no place in politics, and politics had no place in the Church. This didn't seem like the Church in which Jason had grown up, and he wondered if it wasn't so much that he had left the Church, but that the Church had left him.

When things stop making sense, it can seem as if the world is caving in around us. This is especially true in regard to the Church. Apparent incongruence can leave us feeling as though somehow the rug has been pulled out from under us.

The Church has been involved in politics in one way or another since Old Testament times. In spite of the prophet Samuel's warnings that a king would enslave, tax, and send the Israelites to war, they insisted on having a king appointed to reign over them. Saul was chosen king over Israel, and from then on, the Israelites struggled to balance morals and governance.

Jesus himself was caught in a political struggle. He preached the Truth in the Temple on numerous occasions, knowing that eventually his words might incite antagonism. The scribes and Pharisees watched his every move, waiting for the right moment to charge him with blasphemy. The moment finally came late one night in a quiet garden on the Mount of Olives. They captured Jesus and took him to the court of Pontius Pilate. To ensure a conviction, they tried to convince Pilate that Jesus had attempted to incite an insurrection. Pilate knew Jesus was innocent of the charges levied against him and wanted to release him. All Jesus had to do was deny that he was the Son of God, and he would be free. Yet he stood for the Truth, even though he knew that he would suffer a horrifying death at the hands of Roman executioners because of it. Fearing political upheaval and insurgency, Pilate agreed to have Jesus crucified. Finding the correct balance between morality and governance isn't easy for anyone.

What does Scripture say?

But the people refused to listen to the voice of Samuel; they said, "No! but we are determined to have a king over us, so that we also may be like other nations, and that our king may govern us and go out before us and fight our battles." When Samuel had heard all the words of the people, he repeated them in the ears of the Lord. The Lord said to Samuel, "Listen to their voice and set a king over them." Samuel then said to the people of Israel, "Each of you return home."

1 SAMUEL 8:19–22

What does my heart say?

- How do I form my political opinions?
- Why would the Catholic Church care
  about the laws and policies of a particular nation?
- Why might the Israelites have wanted a king
  to reign over them?

~~~~~

Don't Upset Your Mother

As a child and teenager, Roberta had been a devout Catholic. She practiced her faith, attended Mass and reconciliation regularly, and wanted to become a nun when she grew up. On the outside, she seemed like a typical, happy youngster growing up in a typical, happy, Catholic family.

After high school, she entered college and majored in music theory. Then things began to change. There wasn't anything typical or happy about Roberta anymore. She slipped into depression and attempted suicide several times. After each attempt, she tried to rally herself, tried to get reinvolved in the Church, tried to make life seem normal again. It wouldn't.

On her last attempt, she went into a coma. A priest came, gave her the anointing of the sick, and prayed over her. Her mother had died some years before, but someone had saved her rosary and hung it on Roberta's bedpost. When she awoke, her nurse explained to her all that had happened while she'd been comatose. Then the nurse gave her a card with a prayer to Saint Luke.

"You won't make it if you keep going on this way," the nurse said. Roberta knew she was right.

She began seeing a therapist and had conversations with several priests. She went to Mass occasionally, but was frequently turned off by the homilies. One in particular really bothered her.

"The priest seemed so anti-gay," she said. "A lot of my friends were gay, and yet they had great relationships with their partners. Most of them had suffered sexual abuse as children and only felt safe with another woman."

There was another, underlying reason Roberta had difficulty with the sermons. She, too, had suffered abuse as a child. Her mother suffered from serious mental illness, and the family members had to watch their every move lest they do something to set her off. Roberta remembers frequent warnings from her father not to do anything that would upset her mother.

One of Roberta's most vivid memories of her mother occurred when she was very young and had gotten into some kind of trouble. Her mother commanded her to kneel down on the floor and ask God's forgiveness for what she had done. Her mother told her that the ground was going to open and the devil would come out to swallow her up. All the while, she was beating Roberta with a belt.

As a result of her childhood abuse, Roberta suffers from a dissociative disorder that causes her to assume alternate identities. She doesn't easily get close to others and has difficulty with physical intimacy. Her therapist has been able to help her live a productive life. But her search for an opening back into the Church continues. She wants more than anything to find a way to share her gift for music, but she never seems to quite fit in. Each time she thinks she's found the Church entrance, something keeps her from walking through.

Childhood abuse of any kind can leave us feeling lost, inadequate, and disconnected from those around us. It can even leave us disconnected from ourselves. When the abuse involves religious practices and concepts used as threats or punishments, we can develop an aversion to the Catholic faith rather than to the abuse itself. The rituals that should bring us peace and comfort instead dredge up fear and bad memories. This can place a wall between us and the Church—a wall that can only be scaled through patience, determination, and the grace of God.

What does Scripture say?

Then little children were being brought to him in order that he might lay his hands on them and pray. The disciples spoke sternly to those who brought them; but Jesus said, "Let the little children come to me, and do not stop them; for it is to such as these that the kingdom of heaven belongs." And he laid his hands on them and went on his way.

MATTHEW 19:13–15

What does my heart say?

- How has my childhood affected my view of the Catholic Church?
- What part of my past is holding me back from deepening my faith?
- How can I allow myself to become a child in Jesus' presence, to allow him to lay his hands on me?

vvvvvv

Men in Long, Black Dresses

Angie could feel her blood begin to boil. Slowly the anger built inside of her, like a volcano that could no longer be contained. She could barely sit still in the pew as she listened to the homily that Sunday. The pastor was talking about abortion, describing the process and its effects on the fetus, delineating the teaching of the Church and its reasons for forbidding abortion.

How dare he tell me what to do with my body, Angie fumed. What does he know about unwanted pregnancy? He's never been pregnant, and he never will be. All he does all day is wander around in that long dress of his telling everybody what to do.

Angie couldn't take any more. The incongruity of the situation spun her into a raging fury. She didn't want to listen to this man who seemed so removed from the real world. Who was he to tell her what to do with her own body? He had no right to say what he was saying. She scooted to the end of her pew, rose, ignored the eyes of her fellow parishioners, and walked out of the church. She never went back.

Few of us have an innate inclination to accept authority, particularly when we think that we have nothing in common with the person exercising that authority. We say, "If you haven't walked in my shoes, how can you tell me which steps to take in them?" It's even more difficult when the authority comes from a source that we feel has no business in our private lives. We simply don't like to be told what to do.

Sometimes, however, we need to be told what to do. Our human reasoning isn't perfect, and we can wander into treacherous situations without even being aware that we're in danger.

There's nothing I dislike more than being told what to do. The spirit of obedience doesn't come naturally to me. I've always been the kind of person who likes to figure things out for myself, who ends up learning everything the hard way, who tends to experience the wrong turns before finding the right path.

After my father died, my brother—eleven years older than me— tried to offer me some guidance. I was just fifteen years old, and I rebuffed every bit of advice and scoffed at every admonition. How could he know what it was like to be a fatherless, fifteen-year-old girl? What gave him the right to tell me what to do with my life?

I remember my brother urging me to attend college in Milwaukee rather than stay at home and attend the local community college as I'd planned. I ignored his recommendation and went to the community college anyway. Only later did I realize the folly of my stubbornness. I ended up in a relationship that held me back rather than helped me grow and wasted time on credits that didn't transfer into my major.

My brother wasn't trying to tell me what to do just for the sake of telling me what to do. He was trying to guide me away from a situation that could cause me harm and affect my future, because he was able to see things from a different perspective.

So it is with the Church. The Church stands against abortion because every human has an inalienable right to life, and that life must be respected and protected absolutely from the moment of conception until death. What's more, the Church seeks to protect not only the lives of unborn children, but all life—yours and mine. Our priests and bishops don't tell us what to do just for the sake of telling us what to do. They see things from a different perspective than we do and are trying to guide us away from situations that could cause us harm and affect our future—our eternal future.

What does Scripture say?

> When he entered the temple, the chief priests and the elders of the people came to him as he was teaching, and said, "By what authority are you doing these things, and who gave you this authority?"
>
> MATTHEW 21:23

What does my heart say?

- ° How do I respond to authority in my life?
- ° Do I see the Church as a valid authority? Why or why not?
- ° When have I rebuffed authority and regretted it later?

∿∿∿∿

Like Nun Other

Betty was the daughter of Eastern European immigrants. Her parents had suffered at the hands of the Nazis in World War II and were sponsored by a West Coast Jewish family to come to the United States. They hadn't much more to live on than their Catholic faith and their determination.

Still, they managed to send Betty to a Catholic grade school run by an order of teaching nuns. The family spoke their native language at home, giving Betty a distinctive accent that was a point of contention in postwar America. At school, she was considered an oddity and had difficulty making friends. Being scorned by the other children was bad enough, but Betty also felt scorned by the nuns. It seemed that they were always finding reasons to punish her and make her feel bad about herself. She witnessed other students receiving the same treatment and older nuns verbally abusing younger nuns in front of the students.

One day, it became too much for Betty. A nun lost her temper and called another student a "stupid diabetic" because the student was having difficulty understanding math and also had diabetes. Betty lost her temper. She stood up and reprimanded the nun for her behavior. The nun grabbed her by the neck and threw her out of the classroom. At that same moment, the pastor happened to walk past the classroom. The nun told him Betty was being insubordinate and should be expelled. After a private conversation with Betty, the pastor disciplined the teacher. But the damage had already been done: From that point forward, Betty began her journey away from the Catholic Church.

Insult was added to injury when another nun, presumably suffering from dementia, replaced the regular teacher. She told the students that if children put their hand over a burning candle and it burned, it meant they were sinners and that night the devil would come and get them. She also told them that the devil would come at night and take evil children to hell if they didn't wear a rosary around their necks to bed. She told them that she once saw a boy who did not wear his rosary at night touch a curtain and set it on fire with his bare hands. To a rational person, these stories are absurd. To a young girl taught to honor and respect religious women, it was gospel truth. For years after that, Betty was afraid to be alone in the house for fear the devil would come to get her.

Not all of Betty's encounters with nuns were so shocking. Some of them were quite pleasant, like the nuns who ran the hospital where her mother worked. They kindly cared for Betty during her mother's shifts, made her paper nurse's hats, and let her visit the children in the pediatric unit. Sometimes, they allowed her to watch Archbishop Fulton Sheen on television with them. Betty enjoyed being with those nuns.

Through high school and college, Betty tried to maintain her affiliation with the Catholic Church, marrying a Catholic man in a Catholic church, sending her own two children to Catholic grade school, and joining the local parish. The final straw came when her husband was laid off. The parish pastor stopped into the discount store where Betty worked. He recognized her, and they chatted while she waited on him. When Betty told him about her husband, his interest level didn't seem to change at all. Betty was hurt and offended.

She decided to try out the church her neighbors attended. It wasn't Catholic, but at this point it was more important to find a pastor and congregation that would nurture her family. Betty and her family liked what they saw and stayed. Betty often misses the rituals and traditions of the Catholic Church, but her negative experiences hold her back from rejoining.

We're all like that in one way or another, aren't we? We're a bit like the dogs in Pavlov's famous experiment. He was able to elicit a particular behavior from them by repeating a stimulus. If we've been conditioned by certain experiences, it's difficult to recondition ourselves to work past them.

Perhaps we can find consolation in the Book of Job. Job was tested by God and scorned by family and friends. Yet he remained faithful through every rebuff, steadfast through every trial. He didn't give up on God, because he knew God wouldn't give up on him. People will pass away in time; God will not. Faithfulness is a gift for which we all must pray.

What does Scripture say?

"O earth, do not cover my blood; let my outcry find no resting place. Even now, in fact, my witness is in heaven, and he that vouches for me is on high. My friends scorn me; my eye pours out tears to God, that he would maintain the right of a mortal with God, as one does for a neighbor. For when a few years have come, I shall go the way from which I shall not return."

JOB 16:18–22

What does my heart say?

- ° What does Job mean by
  "I shall go the way from which I shall not return?"
- ° How has my attitude toward the Church been conditioned?
- ° Is there something about the rituals and traditions
  of the Church that I miss? What is it?

∿∿∿∿

Annulled or Not Annulled?

Virginia hasn't received the Eucharist in fifty-one years. She goes to Mass on Sundays, but doesn't get into the Communion line because she believes she isn't allowed to receive the Eucharist. She married a non-Catholic man who is divorced from his first wife. His first marriage was annulled by his church, but, according to their understanding, the Catholic Church doesn't recognize it as a valid declaration of matrimonial nullity. At the time of their marriage, Virginia and her fiancé loved each other and couldn't imagine life apart from one another. They didn't see any other options, so they were married by a justice of the peace. Since then, Virginia has considered herself a lapsed Catholic.

Why does she continue to attend Mass? As a child, she was told that the Catholic faith is the one true faith, and she believes that. She was raised in a divorced family; her father was Catholic and her mother was Lutheran. Yet her mother raised her Catholic, scraping together the tuition to send her to a Catholic grade school. She received her first holy Communion in second grade, was confirmed in sixth grade, and sang in the parish choir. Eventually, the cost became too much for Virginia's mother, and she had to withdraw her daughter from the Catholic grade school and place her in the public school system. Virginia then entered the religious education program at her parish and subsequently spent seventeen years as a teacher in the program. In spite of her valiant efforts to provide her daughter with a Catholic education, Virginia's mother remained a Lutheran. She explained this to Virginia by telling her that God is neither Catholic nor Lutheran; God is simply God.

But Virginia still loved her Catholic faith. That's why she raised her own child Catholic and paid for the Catholic education of her grandchildren. She's convinced that the Catholic faith's greatest force is the values it gives to children.

In the early years of her marriage, Virginia sought advice about her marital situation from various sources. Somehow she got the impression that there was no way for her to reconcile her marriage with the Church, and that she and her husband were considered unworthy and adulterers. She doesn't think she'll ever be welcomed back into the Catholic Church and has decided to continue practicing her Catholic faith in her own way, as best she can. She's confused and angry. She's resolved to cling to the hope that God will hear her prayer and will forgive what she believes the Church will not.

The Church does forgive Virginia and her husband. While it's true that the Catholic Church doesn't accept the marriage dissolutions of other denominations, it does provide means for an individual married and divorced in another faith tradition to file for a declaration of invalidity with the Metropolitan Tribunal. The process involves an examination of the situation to determine whether a marriage truly existed. Once a decision is reached, and if it is an affirmative decision in regard to nullity, the individual is free to marry. Had Virginia and her husband sought the assistance of their Tribunal, they could have obtained a declaration of nullity for her husband's first marriage, had their marriage blessed in the Catholic Church, and received the Eucharist for the past five decades. The Church doesn't close off those with difficult marital situations. Rather, it offers the means by which full communion with the Church may be regained through its tribunals.

At times, things aren't as clear as we'd like them to be. Explanations don't make sense, laws seem unjust, counselors misdirect us, and contradictions surround us. God could have made it all so simple. Why, instead, did God make it so complicated?

It's been complicated since the Fall. When Adam and Eve refused God's will in the Garden of Eden, it made the whole world complicated for all of us. Our human efforts to restore order aren't always successful. The closest we can come to simplifying things is our Catholic faith. The Church in its wisdom seeks to guide us, not for the sake of making us feel unworthy, but rather for the sake of assuring our salvation. Its laws aren't arbitrary and vindictive; they're formed in wisdom and prayerful discernment. We might not always agree with them, but we will always benefit from them.

What does Scripture say?

"The days are surely coming, says the Lord, when I will establish a new covenant with the house of Israel and with the house of Judah; not like the covenant that I made with their ancestors, on the day when I took them by the hand to lead them out of the land of Egypt; for they did not continue in my covenant, and so I had no concern for them, says the Lord. This is the covenant that I will make with the house of Israel after those days, says the Lord: I will put my laws in their minds, and write them on their hearts, and I will be their God, and they shall be my people. And they shall not teach one another or say to each other, 'Know the Lord,' for they shall all know me, from the least of them to the greatest. For I will be merciful toward their iniquities, and I will remember their sins no more."

HEBREWS 8:8–12

What does my heart say?

- What rules or guidelines have I had to make that others didn't immediately understand?
- How would I define "covenant?"
  With whom do I share a covenant?
- What does "I will be their God, and they shall be my people" mean to me?

~~~~~

Resurrecturis

Amber sat in the car waiting for her mother to leave work. As she was sitting there thinking, her eyes wandered to the cemetery across the street. She was struck by the word *Resurrecturis* inscribed on the big cemetery archway, and she tried to translate it. She discovered that the meaning is "for those about to revive." She thought about it for a long time. *Yeah right*, she said to herself. Something about the experience of that day made her lose all hope in the resurrection. This, combined with a sense of general hopelessness, depression, chaos, and entropy is the reason she first stopped going to church.

A year later—her senior year in college—she tried to reclaim her Catholic identity. She was successful to some extent. She went on retreat, received reconciliation, and started attending Mass again. Slowly, through prayer and reflection, she felt as if she were finding her way back to genuinely practicing her Catholic faith. It didn't last.

As she looked around at other young adults in the Church, she became more and more disturbed by the discrepancy between the Church's teachings regarding human sexuality and the practices of many Catholics. It appeared to her that the Church promoted only confusion, guilt, scruples, addictions, and radical denial and hypocrisy rather than encourage the development of a healthy sexuality prior to, or perhaps even within, marriage. Her friends beginning Catholic marriage preparation were perfectly comfortable with never addressing their history of premarital sex or their intentions to use birth-control pills, condoms, or even Plan B contraceptives if necessary, until they decided to eventually have children. She saw others addicted to masturbation, who confessed it every week in reconciliation, but then went back to masturbating, unable to break free of the cycle of "obsession". It seemed to her that her peers either ignored the teachings of the Church completely or were caught in a state of obligation arising from guilt and ignorance, unable to live freely and contented with their choice.

Amber's lifestyle and views changed. She no longer agreed with the Church's strictures on sexuality, which she considered an utter quashing of any sexual urges outside of procreation. Rather than confess something dishonestly week after week, she decided to simply stop receiving Communion. Although she continues to attend Sunday Mass, she feels that the Church has buried its head in the sand and is behind the times. She's eagerly waiting for a new model of sexuality to appear.

It's no wonder Amber and so many other young adults feel a sense of hopelessness, chaos, and entropy. They're caught between a world that changes exponentially with each passing moment—spewing relativism and obscuring truth—and a Church that attempts to provide a solid foundation with consistent morality. The Church's perspective isn't always the most popular one, but it is the most stable one. The faster the world moves, the greater the challenge for the Church to address the arising issues with the right mix of solid teaching and pastoral care.

Regardless of approach, however, the Church can never stray from the commands given by God. If the Church altered its doctrines and structures in the same manner that the world around it does, it would lose the trust and respect of not only its own people, but also of other religions and institutions worldwide. The Church may change its approach, but it may never change the Truth.

Jesus said this when he proclaimed the kingdom of God. He told the crowds who had come to listen to him that he had come not to abolish the law or the prophets but to fulfill them. Jesus did not change the law for the people; he changed the people for the law. The Church teaches us to sanctify our sexual identity, not to deny it. It also teaches that our sexual identity involves much more than our reproductive organs. It encompasses our entire being, body and soul. It especially concerns our capacity to love, participate in creation, and form lasting bonds.

Here's what the *Catechism of the Catholic Church* says: "Everyone, man and woman, should acknowledge and accept his sexual identity. Physical, moral, and spiritual difference and complementarity are oriented toward the goods of marriage and the fortune of family life. The harmony of the couple and of society depends in part on the way in which the complementarity, needs, and mutual support between the sexes are lived out" (2333).

The Church does not want to stifle our sexuality; it wants to enhance it and protect it from becoming selfish and vile. The Church can't change its laws to make us float more easily on the waves of popular culture. It has to remain steadfast so that we don't go under and drown.

What does Scripture say?

"Do not think that I have come to abolish the law or the prophets; I have come not to abolish but to fulfill. For truly I tell you, until heaven and earth pass away, not one letter, not one stroke of a letter, will pass from the law until all is accomplished. Therefore, whoever breaks one of the least of these commandments, and teaches others to do the same, will be called least in the kingdom of heaven; but whoever does them and teaches them will be called great in the kingdom of heaven. For I tell you, unless your righteousness exceeds that of the scribes and Pharisees, you will never enter the kingdom of heaven."

MATTHEW 5:17–20

What does my heart say?

- ○ Why did God give Moses the Ten Commandments?
- ○ What did Jesus mean when he said that he had come to fulfill the law?
- ○ What do I expect from the Church in terms of guidance for my life?

⌇⌇⌇⌇⌇

Disillusioned by Scandal

In 2002, it was discovered that William's archbishop had paid a large sum of archdiocesan money to settle a sexual assault claim against him, a fact he'd concealed for more than two decades. This was at the height of the sex-abuse scandals in the Catholic Church, and it seemed to William that the entire Church was imploding before his eyes.

Other things added to his disillusionment. A priest he'd known as a child was removed from the priesthood after allegations of pedophilia were substantiated against him. Another was found dead in his rectory, a victim of suicide. At another church he attended, the bookkeeper was convicted of gambling away hundreds of thousands of parish dollars. On a personal level, he felt as though the Church were oriented only toward married persons, overemphasizing marriage and family and underemphasizing the value of single individuals such as himself. William just couldn't accept it anymore. He stopped going to Mass.

He still prays every day, reads the Bible occasionally, and reads a Catholic newspaper just to see how things are going. He was brought up to believe that priests had a special calling, and that they received special graces upon ordination that would protect them from scandalous behavior. To William, priests were examples to be admired and emulated. It was a devastating blow for him to see that they are as fallible as any layperson, and that they're capable of trying to cover up their own sins. His disillusionment ruptured his relationship with the Church. He feels as though he's connected to God but disconnected from the Church. He wonders if there's any way he'll be able to reconnect.

The entire Catholic Church was rocked by the sex-abuse scandals.

Everyone was affected, from the Holy Father to the people in the pews. There's no denying the severity of the crisis. Many people suffered indescribable pain and trauma at the hands of a few. But we must remember that it was only a few.

A 2002 *Washington Post* survey showed that in the four decades prior to the outbreak of the scandals, less than 1.5 percent of the estimated sixty thousand Catholic clergy members had been accused of sexual abuse. A 2003 *New York Times* survey showed that 1.8 percent of all priests ordained from 1950 to 2001 had been accused of child abuse. Thomas Kane, author of *Priests Are People Too*, estimates that between 1 percent and 1.5 percent of priests have had charges brought against them. These are very small percentages compared to the total number of priests in our country.

It is also important to note that Catholic priests are not the only persons who have been involved in sexual abuse. A 2004 study by the Catholic League for Religious and Civil Rights showed that the incidence of sexual abuse of minors is slightly higher among Protestant clergy than among Catholic clergy, and that it's significantly higher among public-school teachers than among either of these two clerical groups. The study also showed that sexual abuse among Jewish rabbis occurs about as frequently as among Protestant clergy, and between 3 percent and 12 percent of psychologists have had sexual contact with their clients. Sexual abuse is a problem for society in general, not merely for Catholic priests.

Perhaps it also would be helpful to consider the nature of the ordination of Catholic priests. Priestly ordination is a gift, not a right. It's a sacrament conferred on a person willing to answer God's call to serve his people, not a guarantee that the man ordained will be immune to temptation and sin. Through our baptism, we too are called to participate in the priestly, prophetic, and kingly office of

Christ. Are we completely immune from all temptation and sin? Of course not. Then why should we expect our priests to be immune?

Think of whom Christ called to be apostles. They were chosen from among the common people. They weren't highly educated, spiritually exceptional, or free from sin. One was a tax collector. One doubted the credibility of Christ's resurrection. And one denied Christ three times in the hour he most needed him. Yet Christ chose these men to be the foundation of the Catholic Church and gave them responsibility for spreading the Good News throughout the entire world.

The Church has blemishes, but it's not completely rotted. It's made up of human beings who are susceptible to failure. It's a living, breathing organism that is sometimes better, sometimes worse at cooperating with God's plan for our salvation. Our hope remains in the God who created us, in the God who continues to guide us, and in the God who continues to forgive us when we fail.

What does Scripture say?

He went up the mountain and called to him those whom he wanted, and they came to him. And he appointed twelve, whom he also named apostles, to be with him, and to be sent out to proclaim the message, and to have authority to cast out demons. So he appointed the twelve: Simon (to whom he gave the name Peter); James son of Zebedee and John the brother of James (to whom he gave the name Boanerges, that is, Sons of Thunder); and Andrew, and Philip, and Bartholomew, and Matthew, and Thomas, and James son of Alphaeus, and Thaddaeus, and Simon the Cananaean, and Judas Iscariot, who betrayed him.

MARK 3:13–19

What does my heart say?

° When have I been called to take up a task that
I felt incapable of completing?

° Which of the apostles do I most closely relate to?
Matthew, who was a tax collector?
Thomas, who doubted the credibility of the resurrection?
Or Peter, who denied Christ three times? Why?

° Why did Jesus choose the apostles he chose?

Background Noise

Kimberly's decision to leave the Catholic Church wasn't made in anger or frustration. Rather it was made through much prayer and consideration after a series of events affected her view of the Church. She felt she was being led another direction.

As a child, she had many positive experiences in the Catholic Church. Some of her earliest memories are of Vacation Bible School, which offered excitement and a change of pace for the summer. She enjoyed the lessons, the songs, and the time outdoors. As she grew older, she assisted in teaching the younger classes. She enjoyed the rhythm of going to Mass every Sunday and often babysat during the church's small group activities. She was especially impressed by the parish's prayer group, which showed her a type of prayer she had not seen before. They spoke to God from their hearts.

Even so, she began to feel as if something were missing in her life. When it came time to be confirmed in the Catholic Church, she was steeped in questions and doubts. She didn't feel ready to be confirmed, but her parents insisted that she do it. She felt like a liar.

And all along—from elementary school into high school and college—something was playing in the background. In high school, she befriended a girl who came from a strong Catholic family. Her friend introduced her to Christian music, and the family invited her to join them for Scripture readings. As a day-camp counselor for the YMCA, Kimberly was invited to join the Fellowship of Christian Athletes and was attracted to their style of worship and their Bible studies.

At the Catholic college she attended, run by religious sisters, her eyes continued to be open to new things. She saw the beautiful, close relationship the sisters had with the Lord. She saw their humble lives, lived daily for God. She became involved in campus ministry and served a year on the worship planning team. She spent time with her Catholic roommate's family and experienced their prayerful devotion, even in day-to-day activities. She went on a mission trip to Mississippi, serving in soup kitchens and doing charity projects. There she was exposed to the vitality of a black Catholic church, and she loved it.

Her college years, however, raised still more questions. She began to wonder why Catholics do the things they do and what it all meant. She didn't see the point of fasting during Lent and taking the day off on Sundays, as her roommates did. She didn't understand why Catholics seemed to rattle off the same prayers week after week in Mass rather than pray to God spontaneously from their hearts. Her non-Catholic friends started asking her questions about her Catholic faith, questions she couldn't answer. They wanted to know why Catholics worship Mary. They wanted to know why Catholics go to a priest for confession instead of going right to God through Jesus. They wanted to know why there were so many statues in the churches. She didn't know.

Kimberly joined a Bible-study group through another denomination and realized that to establish the relationship with God for which she yearned, she must commit herself to studying the Word and opening her heart to the guidance of the Holy Spirit. She had grown up in a home where the Bible sat on the shelf, so this was a new experience for her. The deeper she dug into the Protestant Bible study, the less sense the prayers, rituals, and traditions of the Catholic Church made to her.

She doesn't see herself going back to the Catholic Church because she feels she's a different person now. She has a relationship with the Lord and an understanding of the Bible she never had before. She says she has no distorted view that all Catholics are headed in the wrong direction, or that all non-Catholics are headed in the right direction. She believes that the Lord does not look at our denominations but at our obedience, our attitude, and our humbleness before God.

Interestingly, the new priest at the Catholic church in town intrigues her. She's heard that people complain about him because they think he's too strict, that he doesn't want people up on the altar, that he doesn't let them chew gum in Mass, that he gets mad if people leave right after Communion, that he has a disdain for young people who live together before marriage, and so on. Kimberly wishes she could tell them, "People! This man is right on track. He's trying to teach you reverence for the Lord. He's doing his best to show you what is healthy and holy in the Lord's eyes. God's laws are there for a reason—because God loves us and wants to protect us!"

Apparently there are components of Kimberly's Catholic upbringing that are still deeply rooted. Did she drift away from the Church because she had been undercatechized as a young person? If she had understood that Catholics venerate, not worship, Mary, that as Christ's mother she is our mother too, she may have been able to better explain Marian devotion to her non-Catholic friends. If she had understood that Mass is biblically based, and that much of Church teaching and tradition is based on the Bible, perhaps she would not have felt something was missing from her faith life. A better grasp of the meaning and importance of sacramentals such as statues may have helped her feel less like an idol worshiper and more like an active participant in the communion of saints. If she had only known that the Church does indeed promote spontaneous individual and group prayer, and that the Mass is the ultimate form of unity rather than rote recital, she may not have felt so disassociated and been attracted to another denomination. Somehow she lost sight of the beauty of the Catholic Church's teachings and the knowledge that they're founded on a combination of Scripture, dogma, and tradition. The roots were there, but the plant wasn't nurtured in the way it needed in order to grow and develop.

What does Scripture say?

He said to them, "But who do you say that I am?" Simon Peter answered, "You are the Messiah, the Son of the living God." And Jesus answered him, "Blessed are you, Simon son of Jonah! For flesh and blood has not revealed this to you, but my Father in heaven. And I tell you, you are Peter, and on this rock I will build my church, and the gates of Hades will not prevail against it. I will give you the keys of the kingdom of heaven, and whatever you bind on earth will be bound in heaven, and whatever you loose on earth will be loosed in heaven."

MATTHEW 16:15–19

What does my heart say?

- ° Which of the rituals, prayers, and traditions
  of the Catholic Church make me feel closest to God? Why?
- ° If I feel I'm missing something in my Catholic faith, what is it?
- ° Do I feel that I have been adequately catechized?
  If not, how can I resolve that?

~~~~~

Born in the Wrong Century

Sometimes Jasper wishes he had been born one hundred years earlier so he would have missed all the changes in the Catholic Church since then. In the autumn of his life, he hopes that he can find his way back to the Church before he dies. He says it's hard enough to come back after having been away; it's especially hard to come back to a Church that is different from the one in which he grew up and loved.

He still considers himself a Catholic, but a poor one. His faith journey is one of fits and starts, with one step back and two steps forward over a series of years. Having attended religious education classes and then Catholic grade school as a child, he knows his *Catechism*—something he attributes to the nun who taught him in seventh grade. He received his first holy Communion and confirmation, but his participation dropped off sharply after he left school. He took his first job and received the sacraments very irregularly.

In his late twenties, however, he came across "The Story of Fatima", and was so moved by the story that he bought a hundred copies and donated them to his local Catholic parish. He temporarily reentered the Church, but only for a short while. Eventually, he fell into a state of sin and drifted away.

At about the age of thirty, his conscience began to bother him, and he somehow got the feeling that he needed to receive reconciliation and go back to Mass. He'd been away for a long time and was very nervous. One Saturday afternoon, he gathered his courage and went to the nearest Catholic church. After all this time, and with sin weighing heavily on his soul, he could wait no longer. He went in, said his prayers, and prepared himself to get in line. There were other people in the church, and they seemed to be going out into the front church lobby to wait. So Jasper followed them. He didn't know what was going on. This was different, confusing, and he was afraid because he didn't know what was going to happen. Everybody was waiting, and after waiting for five or perhaps ten minutes, he lost his nerve and walked out. He drove home. After he went in the house, he broke down and cried because he had really wanted reconciliation. But things were not the same in the Church.

He doesn't know what happened that day, but it was the last time he tried to go to reconciliation. He hates change in general, and it was an even bigger blow to him to see changes in a Church that he was certain would always remain the same. That's the last time Jasper ever entered a church, with the rare exception of a few weddings and funerals.

Jasper wishes that the Church could go back to the way things were. He loved the Latin Mass, the way he could follow along in his Mass Missal, and the way it seemed more proper, more solemn, more sacred, more devout, and above all more holy. To him, its beauty is unequaled. The *Novus Ordo* perplexes him. He doesn't understand the rationale behind receiving Communion in the hand, extraordinary ministers of the Eucharist, guitar music, the sign of peace, or Mass celebrated anywhere but in the church building. He knows that in his current state of sin he isn't able to receive the Eucharist. But how can he reconcile with the Church when he doesn't know how to go to reconciliation? He's considered talking to a priest about these things, but isn't sure it will do much good. If one church is like this, then probably they all are. For Jasper, change is not always good.

A mother observes the flow of life around her and notices that the way the household is arranged no longer suits her growing family. The layout of the furniture is no longer functional, the lamps being used don't provide adequate light, and the rugs are so worn that they could cause someone to slip. She knows that in order for her family to have a truly comfortable home, she must rearrange the furniture, purchase lamps with brighter bulbs, and replace the rugs with new ones that will provide better traction.

She sets to work and slowly makes the necessary changes for the comfort and security of her family. They're a bit hard to get used to at first. Here and there the family stumbles over furniture. Initially the extra light is too bright, but the family soon realizes that they can see much more clearly with the new lamps. While there is some shuffling across the new rugs in the beginning, everyone soon appreciates the firm standing that they provide. The changes required adaptation, but in the end the family was grateful to their mother for having the insight and goodness to change things for their benefit. They felt at home again.

The Catholic Church is such a mother. It's not a vindictive institution that seeks to confound and alienate us by changing for the sake of change. Instead, the Church is a caring mother who seeks what is best for her family. Its goals are to make its children as functional as possible so that we can live in the Light and stand firmly and securely on the Truth. Sometimes that takes a little rearranging.

The Second Vatican Council began on October 11, 1962, after nearly four years of meticulous preparation. The council fathers saw the need to set forth a radically different vision of the Church, one that was more biblical, more historical, more vital, and more dynamic. At the same time, they wished to remain faithful to tradition, to foster all lawfully acknowledged rites, and to serve them in the future. In some cases, the Council saw a need for revision. Even then, they sought to maintain the authority and dignity of each rite.

"The Council also desires that, where necessary, the rites be carefully and thoroughly revised in the light of sound tradition, and that they be given new vigor to meet the circumstances and needs of modern times" (*Constitution on the Sacred Liturgy*, 4).

The changes weren't easy for everyone to accept. The most noticeable ones involved the ministering of the sacraments, especially Mass and reconciliation. Here is what the council fathers said in that regard: "In this restoration, both texts and rites should be drawn up so that they express more clearly the holy things which they signify. Christian people, as far as possible, should be able to understand them with ease and to take part in them fully, actively, and as befits the community" (*Constitution on the Sacred Liturgy*, 21).

Some people feel as though the Catholic Church is not the same church it was before. That couldn't be farther from the truth. The Catholic Church is the same church now and always. It is our loving mother who observes, rearranges, and restores so that we can have a home that is truly welcoming, unifying, functional, and sanctifying.

What does Scripture say?

Before she was in labor she gave birth; before her pain came upon her she delivered a son. Who has heard of such a thing? Who has seen such things? Shall a land be born in one day? Shall a nation be delivered in one moment? Yet as soon as Zion was in labor she delivered her children. Shall I open the womb and not deliver? says the Lord; shall I, the one who delivers, shut the womb? says your God. Rejoice with Jerusalem, and be glad for her, all you who love her; rejoice with her in joy, all you who mourn over her— that you may nurse and be satisfied from her consoling breast; that you may drink deeply with delight from her glorious bosom. For thus says the Lord: I will extend prosperity to her like a river, and the wealth of the nations like an overflowing stream; and you shall nurse and be carried on her arm, and dandled on her knees. As a mother comforts her child, so I will comfort you; you shall be comforted in Jerusalem.

ISAIAH 66:7–13

What does my heart say?

- What is it about change—any change—that I don't like?
- When was the last time I effected a change in my own life?
- What were my reasons for doing so?

~~~~~

Playing God

Darla opened her eyes. She was groggy, and her eyes wouldn't focus, but in spite of that she could make out the figure of her mother standing at the end of her hospital bed.

"Do you think you're playing God?" her mother spewed. "Do you think you're smarter than God? Do you think you know better than Jesus when you're supposed to die?"

Darla has never forgotten that moment or her mother's cutting words. She couldn't believe that a mother could treat her child in such a way. She thought that her mother could've said something like, "Thank God you're all right" or even simply "Hello." Instead, in her own human limitations and grief, her mother used words that caused Darla to turn away from the Church completely.

Darla's mother converted to Catholicism in order to marry a Catholic man. But she became a very zealous convert. After twenty-seven years, Darla's parents divorced, and her mother found solace in becoming active in her parish. She taught religious education, led prayer groups, headed liturgy committees, and was an RCIA sponsor, to name a few.

Darla was ten years old and found herself in the middle of a messy divorce. She felt ignored by everyone in her family except her mother. So naturally she clung to her, and they became very close. It seems to Darla that her mother can be excessive and somewhat delusional. Nonetheless, she was the only person upon whom Darla could depend.

At the end of her first year in college, Darla became clinically depressed and attempted suicide three times. On the third time, she was discovered and hospitalized. Her mother was in Rome volunteering at the Vatican for the 2000 Jubilee. When she heard about her daughter's suicide attempt, she rushed home immediately. But her reaction was not what Darla had hoped for, or what she needed. At that moment, Darla realized that her mother's obsession with the Church and its dogma had turned her into something other than a loving mother.

Darla blamed the Church. She was sure that had her mother not gone headfirst into everything Catholic after the divorce, she wouldn't have been so hurtful. After that incident, Darla spent a few years researching and reading, and spent hours talking with the priest at the Catholic Center at her college. She came to the realization that the *Catechism of the Catholic Church* was her single greatest barrier to her relationship with God. She left the Catholic Church and has not received the Eucharist in almost ten years. She says the moment she decided to find her faith outside the Church she felt a weight lifted from her shoulders, and she doesn't anticipate a desire to return. Bitter and disenchanted, she'd rather not have to deal with anything Catholic ever again.

When one person in a group or organization treats us harshly, we're inclined to develop an aversion to the entire institution. It's a natural reaction to think that, if one of the organization's representatives speaks or acts in a certain way, they all will. Feelings of pain and rejection are easily transferred from one to all. It's a great challenge to see each member as an individual capable of acting independently of the others. This is especially true when the pain and rejection we've experienced comes from a member of the Church.

Some years ago, a trusted friend with whom I'd been working on a project betrayed me. I was devastated and found myself steeped in misery, doubt, fear, and anger. The blow was so lethal that it affected my view of the entire organization and began to spill into my view of the Church. It even affected my view of myself and sent me into a downward spiral that took all my strength and every resource available to me to counteract. Had it not been for a kind, insightful, and wise spiritual advisor, I might have been lost.

I began to heal when I began to understand several things. We are all subject to original sin. No one is exempt except our Blessed Mother. We all carry baggage from the past that shapes our views and influences our actions. We are all limited by our human weakness no matter what our condition, status, or position. We are all subject to Satan's cunning and ceaseless crusade to secure our demise. Finally, a person wearing the badge or credentials of a particular organization is not an adequate representation of the entire institution. This is true of families, of community organizations, of religious orders, of grassroots associations, of government, and of the Church.

God sees everything, even that which lies in the darkest recesses of our hearts and souls. We need not worry about those who have caused us pain or harm; God will see to them in God's own time, in God's own way. We need only remember that the Church teaches the Truth, and the Truth does not change regardless of human failing.

What does Scripture say?

Why do you boast, O mighty one, of mischief done against the godly? All day long you are plotting destruction. Your tongue is like a sharp razor, you worker of treachery. You love evil more than good, and lying more than speaking the truth. Selah You love all words that devour, O deceitful tongue. But God will break you down forever; he will snatch and tear you from your tent; he will uproot you from the land of the living. Selah The righteous will see, and fear, and will laugh at the evildoer, saying, "See the one who would not take refuge in God, but trusted in abundant riches, and sought refuge in wealth!" But I am like a green olive tree in the house of God. I trust in the steadfast love of God forever and ever.

I will thank you forever, because of what you have done. In the presence of the faithful I will proclaim your name, for it is good.

PSALM 52

What does my heart say?

- What holds me back from truly forgiving those who have hurt me? What holds me back from allowing others to truly forgive me?
- When have my own shortcomings caused me to harm someone else?
- What does it mean to be an olive tree in the house of God? What does my olive tree look like?

〰〰〰

Hands Down

Stephanie left the Church when she pointed out to an assistant pastor that holding hands during the Our Father was not in accordance with the *General Instruction of the Roman Missal* (*GIRM*). After the *Constitution on the Sacred Liturgy,* issued after the Second Vatican Council, the *GIRM* is the principal liturgical document of the Church that deals with the prayerful celebration of the Eucharist. Both documents are of great importance in that they guide those in charge of liturgical planning. Stephanie takes these documents seriously, and so she felt obligated to draw the assistant pastor's attention to the disparity between the document and her parish's practice.

The assistant pastor replied with what Stephanie felt was an uncharitable response, stating that she was violating Pope John Paul II's Apostolic Exhortation *Reconciliatio et Paenitentia* (Reconciliation and Penance), a letter addressed to bishops, clergy, and laity on reconciliation and penance in the mission of the Church today. Stephanie looked up the letter and could not find any reference in it to holding hands at the Our Father, nor had she ever seen any Pope hold hands at the Our Father during Masses they had celebrated. She left the Church that day.

To her it seemed that this priest was deeply lacking in both formation and tact. If he was the "new" face of the Church, she no longer wished to participate. She says she would be more than happy to come back if someone in authority would correct priests' behavior in regard to handholding at the Our Father, and would further educate all Catholics via announcement at every Mass in every parish and in every bulletin that handholding at the Our Father is not required and is based solely on personal preference. She wants the rights of those who do not want to participate to be honored. She feels that holding hands during the Our Father is a false sign of unity that supplants both the right of peace and the Eucharist that follows.

Stephanie's dilemma is a common one. It can be distressing for a faithful Catholic to attend a Mass or other sacrament that doesn't follow the rubrics. It can make them feel as though the foundation has been pulled out from under them when canon law is distorted or misconstrued. It can be a jolt to their consciences when they're urged to follow a practice that strays from the norms set by the Holy See.

On the other hand, priests don't intentionally lead laity astray. They want what's best for their congregations, while at the same time, they try to meet their parishioners' ever-changing needs, demands, and preferences. Enthusiasm can lead to misrepresentation. Lack of knowledge can lead to unintended infractions. Zeal can lead to abandon.

In many ways, the Catholic Church is still suffering fallout from the Second Vatican Council. The revision of old norms and the proposal of new ones have been repeatedly misinterpreted, making some areas of the sacramental practices seem gray. Clergy and laity alike must take it upon themselves to become educated in these matters so that we can guide one another toward greater understanding and unity.

Neither the Holy See nor the United States Council of Catholic Bishops has officially addressed the question of holding hands during the Lord's Prayer. However, the procedures for the Mass clearly state that the priest and any concelebrant is to pray the Our Father with hands extended, which immediately rules out handholding for them. Spontaneous handholding among the congregation during the Lord's Prayer doesn't present any difficulty. Requiring all those present to do so could cause problems, as it doesn't work well in large groups and can detract from the importance and meaning of the embolism ("Deliver us...") prayed by the priest, the doxology ("For the kingdom...") prayed by the people, and the sign of peace, which follows shortly thereafter.

According to canon law (*Code of Canon Law*, 846), the liturgical books approved by competent authority are to be observed faithfully. No one may add, omit, or alter anything in them on one's own authority. The minister must celebrate the sacraments according to the minister's own rite. In this case, it's the Roman Catholic rite, and the *General Instruction of the Roman Missal* is to be followed exactly.

Regardless of where we stand on the issue of handholding during the Lord's Prayer or any of the other thousands of beautiful and meaningful rituals and traditions of our faith, we all have one thing in common: We love the Church and want to feel at home in its arms.

What does Scripture say?

"And whenever you pray, do not be like the hypocrites; for they love to stand and pray in the synagogues and at the street corners, so that they may be seen by others. Truly I tell you, they have received their reward. But whenever you pray, go into your room and shut the door and pray to your Father who is in secret; and your Father who sees in secret will reward you. "When you are praying, do not heap up empty phrases as the Gentiles do; for they think that they will be heard because of their many words. Do not be like them, for your Father knows what you need before you ask him.

"Pray then in this way: Our Father in heaven, hallowed be your name. Your kingdom come. Your will be done, on earth as it is in heaven. Give us this day our daily bread. And forgive us our debts, as we also have forgiven our debtors. And do not bring us to the time of trial, but rescue us from the evil one. For if you forgive others their trespasses, your heavenly Father will also forgive you; but if you do not forgive others, neither will your Father forgive your trespasses."

MATTHEW 6:5–15

What does my heart say?

- ° What rituals and traditions are important to me in my own life? Why?
- ° Why do I think the Church has established norms for the ministering of the sacraments? How does this affect its people?
- ° What does Jesus mean when he says, "...and your Father who sees in secret will reward you?"

Media Priests

Kenneth headed for the Church exit sometime in 1997 when a new pastor replaced the one who had been at his parish since it was established. The new pastor seemed more like a "media" priest, one who brought all the latest innovations into the Mass, including hand-holding, laughing, clapping, and baptizing. He saw an insincere man with his own agenda, a man whose homilies were long, empty, and focused on Church history but never related to the problems of sin in the world today. Kenneth thought the pastor's aim was to dazzle the members of the congregation with his personality to promote the building of a new church. The priest held "listening" sessions at parishioners' homes, but from what Kenneth understood, the priest did all the talking. A new church was built, one that included a baptismal pool—something with which Kenneth strongly disagreed. So he packed up his family, left the parish, and never looked back.

He found another Catholic parish pastored by a priest who celebrated the liturgy in a very simple and straightforward manner and with a decided focus on the Eucharist. Then something started to happen at his new parish. The formerly part-time volunteer positions of music director and director of religious education were replaced with full-time paid positions filled by people who seemed to have the same zest for innovation as the pastor at Kenneth's old parish. Soon the pastor at his new parish was replaced by a former vicar for clergy who had served under a controversial bishop.

The new pastor effected many changes that were troubling to Kenneth including replacing the quiet, contemplative liturgy with what Kenneth calls a full-blown media event lasting seventy-five minutes; adding even more full-time employees; and running bulletin announcements for a grassroots organization that supported same-sex marriage called Parents, Families and Friends of Lesbians and Gays. Kenneth worked for five years to stop the promotion of this group in his parish and was finally successful.

In Kenneth's opinion, the revelry during Mass increased dramatically, as did a multitude of infractions of the *General Instruction of the Roman Missal*, including holding hands during the Lord's Prayer; vacating of the sanctuary by the priest during the sign of peace; unnecessary addition of both species of Communion; the use of glass decanters and vessels; and the pouring of the precious Blood by a lay minister. Even more disappointing to Kenneth was the fact that visiting priests—including the rector of his diocesan seminary—went along with these infractions.

Kenneth was also perturbed by the pastor's "joke of the week" and the way in which the pastor and assistant pastor took turns poking fun at each other. The fact that the pastor professed to be a "big fan" of a controversial bishop and named a room in the parish annex after him did not help either. Another former vicar for clergy recently replaced this pastor, but Kenneth considers the new one to be similarly arrogant, egotistical, and extremely political. And the infractions continue. Kenneth says that the new priest's homilies are boring, banal, and have no message whatsoever, although they seem to be focused on history and philosophy (as were his predecessor's).

Beneath this layer of troublesome issues with pastors, liturgy, and parish administration lay the sex-abuse scandals which included Kenneth's former bishop. As Kenneth puts it, the scandals turned his stomach against organized religion. Kenneth believes that a concerted effort is under way to perpetuate liturgical abuses and superfluous "stuffing" of the Mass, and that this is the result of misuse and misinterpretation of the documents of the Second Vatican Council. He cites this effort as the main factor in his leaving the Catholic Church.

While he still attends Mass every Sunday, Kenneth goes only for the Eucharist and attends a variety of parishes in an effort to avoid the infractions and practices that he has experienced at his home parish. He refuses to give a single cent more to his diocese than he did ten years ago, even though its financial needs are much greater. Instead he gives his money to Catholic entities in other states. He's given serious consideration to joining a schismatic group, but is holding off in hopes that things will get better in the Roman Catholic Church. He prays for a cessation of liturgical abuses, the resolution of the sex-abuse scandals, and that one day he will again participate fully in the Mass with enthusiasm and conviction.

We must all pray for the Church, not just once in a while but every single day. Our bishops and priests carry a heavy burden and bear a tremendous responsibility in their ministry to the people of God. They worry about cultivating our enthusiasm for the Mass and about guiding the Church so that it is capable of holding its own in a fast-paced and transient culture, while at the same time providing a rock-solid foundation to which we can cling. Sometimes it's difficult to remember that "new" isn't always better, and that "old" doesn't always lead to stagnation.

What does Scripture say?

You shall set the altar of burnt offering before the entrance of the tabernacle of the tent of meeting, and place the basin between the tent of meeting and the altar, and put water in it. You shall set up the court all around, and hang up the screen for the gate of the court. Then you shall take the anointing oil, and anoint the tabernacle and all that is in it, and consecrate it and all its furniture, so that it shall become holy. You shall also anoint the altar of burnt offering and all its utensils, and consecrate the altar, so that the altar shall be most holy. You shall also anoint the basin with its stand, and consecrate it. Then you shall bring Aaron and his sons to the entrance of the tent of meeting, and shall wash them with water, and put on Aaron the sacred vestments, and you shall anoint him and consecrate him, so that he may serve me as priest. You shall bring his sons also and put tunics on them, and anoint them, as you anointed their father, that they may serve me as priests: and their anointing shall admit them to a perpetual priesthood throughout all generations to come.

EXODUS 40:6–15

What does my heart say?

- ° What is my concept of priesthood?
- ° What is the relationship between Aaron's priesthood and the Catholic priesthood of today?
- ° How are Catholic priests anointed today?
  What are the symbols and meaning of that anointing?

2

Taking the
Myway

It always grieved me that some of the most important people in my life had lapsed in their Catholic faith. Knowing that they were no longer receiving the sacraments drove me crazy. Where would they end up without reconciliation? What would happen to their souls without the Eucharist to sustain them? If they stopped believing in the Truth, what would they believe in? I worried about them night and day, nearly to the point of making myself sick.

During a consultation, I poured my heart out about this situation to my spiritual advisor. I just couldn't stand it anymore! Praying wasn't enough. I wanted to do something to bring them back to the Church. Then my spiritual advisor gave me some sound advice.

First, he said, praying is doing something. It's doing more than something—it's keeping the names and faces of my loved ones in constant petition before God. Second, he suggested that each time I receive the Eucharist, I "send" Jesus to my loved ones, asking our Lord to allow them, through me, to receive him in whatever way is theologically possible. They wouldn't physically receive his Body, Blood, Soul, and Divinity, but who knows how Jesus would be present to them and in them. He can do anything! I was greatly consoled and put my spiritual advisor's advice into practice immediately, remaining faithful to it. If they won't go on their own, by golly, I'll go for them.

People stay away from the Church for various reasons. Sometimes it's for one monumental reason that suddenly severed the relationship, and sometimes it's for a collection of smaller reasons that built up over time. Others gradually drift away, seemingly without any reason at all. All of them are looking for something, even though they may not know what it is they're seeking, and their search takes time, patience, and prayer. Those who are seeking mustn't lose hope; those of us praying for them must never tire.

The stories in this chapter are about people who took the "my-way"—the road that led them along a path forged by their own willpower and initiative. They kept traveling that way—often for several years, sometimes for several decades—until the right door was opened, the right resource was found, the right invitation extended… or enough prayers had been said.

〰〰〰

Not Now!

In 1959, Lori went to see her parish priest about baptizing her newborn baby. During the consultation, the priest held Lori's hand for what she felt was an inordinately long time. It made her feel confused and embarrassed, and for years she wondered if her baby had truly been baptized. This was an easy excuse for her to stop going to Mass, and she stayed away from the Church for thirty years, divorcing her husband, raising her daughter, and living the life of a single person. As an independent woman, she bought into the women's liberation movement and enjoyed the freedom and lifestyle that came with it.

During that time, she knew that God was calling her back, but she refused to listen. She describes God's repeated call as the "Hound of Heaven" pursuing her, trying to get her attention. But she always responded with, "Not now!" On one occasion, she attended a presentation at the local Catholic church, which ended with reconciliation. She felt a strong urge to receive the sacrament, but was too embarrassed to admit that she had been away from the Church for such a long time and had "horrible" sins to confess. In spite of her resistance, God would not rest. He called her back to church again, and this time she went to confession. Unfortunately, her "return" did not last very long, but the ground had been prepared, and God had planted the seed for her return. It would take many more years before that seed grew.

In the mid-eighties, Lori decided to give it another try and started attending Mass again. She wanted to test the waters further, so she joined the choir even though she had a "congregation voice" with no range. She even asked the pastor about the possibilities for a divorced woman joining a group in the Church. He told her that she could participate in any group but could not receive the Eucharist since she was living with her fiancé. So she joined and made many new friends.

Some of her new friends were members of the charismatic movement, and they invited her to attend a prayer service with them. Although she was very uncomfortable and thought it weird, she decided to attend a Life in the Spirit seminar, pledging that she would be "out of there" at the first weird thing they did. Despite her fears, the seminar was the impetus she needed to turn her life over to God and return to the Church. She told her fiancé that he had to move out, and the relationship eventually dissolved. A series of very powerful occurrences followed, culminating in her reception of the Eucharist at Pope John Paul II's Mass in New Orleans in 1987.

Since then, she's been a very active Catholic and has taken positions of leadership in the RCIA and Catholics Returning Home programs. She's become an extraordinary minister of the Eucharist, a lector, and part of her parish welcome team. Over time, she was introduced to a rosary apostolate and has found her charism in that ministry.

Lori's own restlessness lured her away from the Church—a restlessness she hoped would be abated by the promises and agenda of political feminism. Instead, she became even more restless than she was before, following a path away from God instead of toward God. What she thought she needed was freedom from God, but what she really needed was freedom for God.

Could it be that we sometimes blame the Church for something that we lack within ourselves? Joining organizations and movements that promise we can have it all usually ends up giving us little or nothing in the long run. We can become so determined to pursue our personal goals that we refuse to listen when God calls us.

What does Scripture say?

Answer me when I call, O God of my right! You gave me
   room when I was in distress. Be gracious to me, and hear
   my prayer.

How long, you people, shall my honor suffer shame? How
   long will you love vain words, and seek after lies? Selah

But know that the Lord has set apart the faithful for himself;
   the Lord hears when I call to him.

When you are disturbed, do not sin; ponder it on your beds,
   and be silent. Selah

Offer right sacrifices, and put your trust in the Lord.

There are many who say, "O that we might see some good!

Let the light of your face shine on us, O Lord!"

You have put gladness in my heart more than when their
grain and wine abound.

I will both lie down and sleep in peace; for you alone, O
Lord, make me lie down in safety.

PSALM 4

What does my heart say?

- What kind of restlessness am I experiencing?
- What's causing or contributing to it?
- What does the Psalmist mean by
  "...the LORD has set apart the faithful for himself..."?

Kicking and Screaming

Ariel is a reverted convert. Raised Methodist, she entered the Catholic Church in 1985. She did not have a firm foundation in her Catholic faith, however, and she believes she was given poor catechesis. She did the bare minimum required of Catholics and eventually fell away from the practice of her faith.

As she looks back, she realizes that the Blessed Virgin Mary has led her most of her life even though, quite frequently, she went kicking and screaming, if at all. She recalls one morning in 1975 when she sat at her kitchen table with an old, broken rosary in her hand, fumbling through a pamphlet on how to pray it. She finally gave up in frustration, because she believed no one could help her.

Sometime after that, a group of Jehovah's Witnesses came to her door. She listened to them and then apologetically dismissed them from her doorstep, claiming she was Catholic and not interested in any other religion. They were so persistent that she finally had to shut the door in their faces. Just before the door closed, they managed to slip in one last comment: They told her that she needed to know the truth.

She had used her Catholic faith as an excuse to get rid of them, but at that moment she realized they had a good point—she really didn't know the Truth. She immediately began to devour the New Testament, reading it five times through but only understanding bits and pieces. One passage in particular stuck with her—the passage in which Jesus tells Peter, "And I tell you, you are Peter, and on this rock I will build my church, and the gates of Hades will not prevail against it" (Matthew 16:18).

One might expect that Ariel would have gone immediately to seek proper instruction in the Catholic faith, but she didn't. Instead, she spent another ten years wandering about, making halfhearted attempts at catechesis, and never following through. It was the death of her mother-in-law in 2001 that finally helped her see the folly of her ways. She experienced an unexpected change of heart and took a trip to a Marian shrine. There she was introduced to the Eternal Word Television Network and the catechetical series of Father John Corapi. She became so inspired by the series that she couldn't get enough Catholic teaching, Catholic history, and Catholic devotion. She was awakened to the lie of the secular culture regarding sexuality, realized her sinfulness, and made her first real confession. She became a consecrated member of a lay missionary society with special devotion to the Immaculate Conception.

It took decades for Ariel to realize that her Catholic faith is the most precious gift God has given her, and that God chose her to serve in a special way by being consecrated to Mary. It's clear that Mary has been raising her as her very own child, preparing her for her life's mission. It's a difficult mission at times, and she must ask for strength to stay on course and not be discouraged. She continues on in spite of her confusion and disappointment with the way things seem to be going in the world. Her path toward her Catholic faith has been long and arduous, but it has been worth every trial.

What does Scripture say?

Therefore, since we are justified by faith, we have peace with God through our Lord Jesus Christ, through whom we have obtained access to this grace in which we stand; and we boast in our hope of sharing the glory of God. And not only that, but we also boast in our sufferings, knowing that suffering produces endurance, and endurance produces character, and character produces hope, and hope does not disappoint us, because God's love has been poured into our hearts through the Holy Spirit that has been given to us.

ROMANS 5:1–5

What does my heart say?

- ○ Where have I wandered in my life?
- ○ Have I ever been discouraged or disappointed with the world around me? When?
- ○ What does it mean to boast in our sufferings?

∿∿∿∿

Not-So-Gently Used

Brenda barely remembers her first holy Communion. The only thing she does remember is that the priest gave a homily about Saint Maria Goretti and said something that she wished she would have more fully understood because it came to have a great bearing on her life.

When she was sixteen, her parents gave her permission to date a seventeen-year-old boy who they had met only once. She didn't really like Jeffrey, but he had been so persistent in asking her out that she went anyway, hoping that agreeing would get him to stop pestering her. Brenda was very naïve and knew little about sexual relationships. Jeffrey asked her to go parking with him and then raped her. Afterward, he apologized and entreated her not to tell anyone because he could go to jail if anyone found out. Then he told her that he really loved her.

Brenda was confused, hurt, scared, and angry. She felt dirty, worthless, sick, and broken. She never told her parents for fear that Jeffrey's threats would come true. Instead of ending the relationship, she continued on because she felt like a used piece of trash and didn't think anyone else would want her. Jeffrey repeatedly abused her sexually, emotionally, and physically. He kept telling her he loved her and made other promises that she knew he'd never keep. Her parents didn't like him, which, in her stubbornness, made her want to stay with him all the more. Her relationship with her parents was strained at best, and her father, the son of an alcoholic mother, was a troubled person.

When confirmation time drew near, Brenda tried to resist, claiming that she was not ready to be confirmed. Deep inside she felt that she could not be confirmed because of the secret with which she was living. During the confirmation retreat, she went to reconciliation and tried to tell the priest what was happening but simply couldn't bring herself to do it. Her parents were insistent, and so she was confirmed.

Jeffrey asked her to marry him on her eighteenth birthday. She didn't want to, but agreed because she felt she had no other option. She was depressed and broken. Her parents were furious when they found out and a huge fight ensued that included physical and verbal abuse from her father. She and Jeffrey decided to elope.

Three weeks before the wedding, Brenda was invited to a graduation party. Her father forced her to go. She got drunk on beer for the first time and, for a short while at least, the beer covered her pain. She met a twenty-one-year-old, Hugh, at the party, but the next day remembered nothing of their conversation. She ran into him a week later. She tried to avoid him because she was embarrassed by her actions (Hugh had taken her home when she was drunk). They met again later at a dance, and her heart stirred. He asked her out on a date, but she tried to put it off. It didn't work. Hugh was different. He was truly interested in Brenda and kept his promises.

Jeffrey stood her up at their elopement, and Brenda was hopeful that things would work out with Hugh. Unfortunately her parents didn't agree. They tried time and again to force her to go back to Jeffrey, despite their earlier disapproval and despite the fact that he insulted her and cursed her to her parents. When Brenda discovered he'd been cheating on her, she broke off the relationship completely.

In spite of the hope that her new relationship with Hugh offered, Brenda began to drink more and more heavily. She had flashbacks and was becoming more and more depressed. Hugh was kind and faithful, and they became sexually involved. Her underlying feelings of worthlessness and pain prohibited her from returning his faithfulness, and she began to live a promiscuous lifestyle, frequenting bars and going home with any man who showed her attention. One night, she decided that there was no meaning to life, and she wanted out of the misery. She tried to commit suicide by overdosing on pills. After she had taken them, she became frightened and ran out into the cornfield near her house. A state patrolman found her running along the highway. He apprehended her and took her to the hospital. She refused to talk to anyone except Hugh; she told him everything.

She ended up getting pregnant, and Hugh proposed to her. He had already purchased an engagement ring and had planned his proposal before he knew she was pregnant. She knew now that his love was real. Slowly, as a couple, they began taking steps to reenter the Church. They attended marriage preparation classes, planned their wedding, and baptized their child in the Catholic Church. They began attending Mass. The more they went, the more they wanted to go.

Six years later, Brenda was driving past a Catholic church with her youngest daughter in the car. It was around six o'clock PM on a Saturday evening, and Mass had just ended. She had no intention of stopping at the church, but she suddenly experienced an inexplicable urge to receive reconciliation. She hadn't been to confession since her confirmation retreat, and she didn't know what to do. The priest was gentle and understanding and led her through the sacrament. She cried uncontrollably and afterward received her penance and absolution. She began meeting with the priest monthly for spiritual direction and began to feel that she was truly forgiven for the terrible secret she had carried in her heart and the sins she had committed over so many years.

She developed an excitement for her Catholic faith that she had never known before. Through a good friend and spiritual mentor, she became affiliated with a Marian movement and consecrated herself to the Blessed Virgin Mary along with the rest of her family. Still she felt something missing from her life. After some searching, she was led to a monastic religious order and attended one of their conferences. There she discovered what she had been missing. She entered the novitiate and became an oblate, and she's happier than she has ever been in her life. She attributes her happiness to two main factors: the prayers of her mother who, in spite of the trials and differences they had in earlier years, prayed the rosary daily for her; second, her realization that when God closes one door, God opens another. God rescued her from an ugly past, gave her another chance at life, and for this she's forever grateful.

Many of us have done things in the past of which we are ashamed. Some of us have lived in wretchedness and debauchery. Some have been led astray by the deceit and wickedness of others. All of us have experienced the effects of sin on our relationship with God in one way or another. Hopefully we also will experience God's boundless goodness and mercy.

What does Scripture say?

Seek the Lord while he may be found, call upon him while he is near; let the wicked forsake their way, and the unrighteous their thoughts; let them return to the Lord, that he may have mercy on them, and to our God, for he will abundantly pardon. For my thoughts are not your thoughts, nor are your ways my ways, says the Lord. For as the heavens are higher than the earth, so are my ways higher than your ways and my thoughts than your thoughts.

For as the rain and the snow come down from heaven, and do not return there until they have watered the earth, making it bring forth and sprout, giving seed to the sower and bread to the eater, so shall my word be that goes out from my mouth; it shall not return to me empty, but it shall accomplish that which I purpose, and succeed in the thing for which I sent it.

ISAIAH 55:6–11

What does my heart say?

- How has my relationship with God been affected by sin?
- Are there others from my past I must learn to forgive? Myself?
- Which of the verses from the book of Isaiah above touch me? In what ways?

〰〰〰

Getting High

Joanie left her Midwest home and traveled to New York City for her freshman year of college, not realizing the university she had chosen was predominantly Jewish. She arrived a week before her roommate and set up half of the dorm room to suit her own tastes. Having gone to Catholic elementary and high schools, she felt proud that her statue of Jesus was on her dresser, there each morning as she got ready for the day. Her roommate arrived and saw Joanie's statue immediately, since it faced the door to the room. She stared at the statue, looked at Joanie with disgust, and said, "I'm Jewish." Joanie shrank. She put Jesus away and began her descent into the world. That was her defining moment, one she faced with a lack of courage rather than defiance.

Her roommate smoked marijuana, so Joanie joined her. She'd never smoked pot before college and discovered that it took her out of herself and gave her a high that she thought was spiritual. She didn't want to be like her roommate, but she wanted her roommate to be her friend. She figured she could always go back to God when she was ready. So marijuana replaced her religion.

Fifteen years of alcohol and marijuana abuse followed. Those two substances were the only "spirituality" Joanie received during that decade and a half. Finally, realizing that things were getting out of hand, she joined Alcoholics Anonymous. The program not only helped her on the road to recovery, but also taught her that she needed spirituality to stay sober.

In an effort to regain what she had lost, she went to a Catholic church on Thanksgiving Day in 2006. At the beginning of the Mass, the pastor said, "and welcome to all our visitors and guests." That one line, said so commonly in Catholic churches everywhere, was the statement Joanie most needed to hear. She didn't want to be a visitor or guest; she wanted to be a full member of the Catholic Church.

She rejoined the Church and has never turned back. She doesn't think that anyone could ever shake her faith again but realizes that test is God's to give. She's now an active member of her parish and is reading the *Catechism of the Catholic Church* cover to cover. She reads Catholic meditations daily, says the rosary, and listens to Relevant Radio frequently. She attends Mass weekly if not more often.

When she looks back, she sees a teenager trapped by peer pressure, people-pleasing, and fear of alienation. She knows these things are what caused her to turn away from God and toward drugs. She thought her highs were spiritual because they gave her a feeling that could only be explained as "out of this world". She knows now that the feeling was only an escape. Her real spirituality doesn't give her a "high", but she does find it "out of this world" because it helps her to actually connect with God. The body, doctrines, prayers, and sacraments of the Catholic Church are her vehicle and guide.

While Joanie now knows that God is not a drug and spirituality is not a high, she realizes that her choices back then were attempts to find God. She is grateful that she didn't feel God's grace until she was sober enough to return to her faith. What's more, she is certain that there are many other young people like her who ignore God's grace and turn to alcohol and drugs as a replacement for religion and spirituality. This is of great concern to her, so she shares her own story of falling away in hopes that it will prevent someone else from doing the same.

What does Scripture say?

Since therefore Christ suffered in the flesh, arm yourselves also with the same intention (for whoever has suffered in the flesh has finished with sin), so as to live for the rest of your earthly life no longer by human desires but by the will of God. You have already spent enough time in doing what the Gentiles like to do, living in licentiousness, passions, drunkenness, revels, carousing, and lawless idolatry.

They are surprised that you no longer join them in the same excesses of dissipation, and so they blaspheme. But they will have to give an accounting to him who stands ready to judge the living and the dead. For this is the reason the gospel was proclaimed even to the dead, so that, though they had been judged in the flesh as everyone is judged, they might live in the spirit as God does.

The end of all things is near; therefore be serious and discipline yourselves for the sake of your prayers. Above all, maintain constant love for one another, for love covers a multitude of sins. Be hospitable to one another without complaining. Like good stewards of the manifold grace of God, serve one another with whatever gift each of you has received. Whoever speaks must do so as one speaking the very words of God; whoever serves must do so with the strength that God supplies, so that God may be glorified in all things through Jesus Christ. To him belong the glory and the power forever and ever. Amen.

1 PETER 4:1–11

What does my heart say?

- ° Am I a leader or a follower?
  Do I fear being alienated from my peers? Why?
- ° What has been my source of spirituality in the past?
  How did that affect my life?
- ° What does my spirituality look like right now?
  On what is it based?

∿∿∿

Homosexual Union

Roger's bishop had been lobbying hard trying to convince voters to vote for the passage of a constitutional amendment that would prevent any legal contract between same-sex couples from being recognized. Simultaneously, as a faithful partner to his same-sex spouse, Roger was working hard to prevent passage of the same amendment.

He bumped into the bishop at a diocesan event and asked him about it. For Roger, the legal contracts between him and his spouse were part of what kept them chaste, holy, and stable. He approached the bishop and asked for his advice. He was expecting either compassion or a lecture but was given neither. Instead he received what he considered to be a dumbfounded silence uncharacteristic of the prelate's usual joviality. The bishop's response made Roger feel as though he didn't matter, as though he were a sheep in the flock that the shepherd would just as soon allow to wander off a cliff.

The next day, Roger joined the Anglican Church. There he felt he was viewed eye-to-eye as a gay man, and he found the music and reverent liturgy much more gratifying than what he had known in the Catholic Church. The beauty of the High Church liturgy enticed him and was a stark contrast to the liturgies offered at his former Catholic parish. In his own words, he states that he existed for forty years with smiling, chatty celebrants accompanied by guitar-strumming musicians and a cantor who came straight from *American Idol*. He loved the incense, hymns, and vestments of the Anglican Church and felt more comfortable with a liturgy that seemed unchanged over the centuries and that he expected would remain unchanged. He felt that, conversely, the Catholic liturgy could be changed on a whim, depending upon what a committee member might decide was relevant…or not. This arbitrariness made him feel angry and unsettled.

After some time in the Anglican Church, however, Roger began to reconsider his Catholic faith. He became curious about the Church's real teachings on human dignity and homosexuality and read the *Catechism of the Catholic Church*. According to his reading, he understood that the Catholic Church welcomed him as a man, welcomed him and his partner as a gay couple, and encouraged them to grow in holiness as partners and helpmates, filled with grace. He decided that the bishops who condemned gay people must have been speaking for themselves and not for the Church.

Roger found a Catholic parish in which Mass was celebrated in Latin and in which they tended to ignore what he saw as the political action initiatives of the Catholic Episcopate. Apart from the occasional prayer offered for the unborn, the focus appeared to be on God and God alone.

Roger feels now that he can finally go to Mass and feel like one of the faithful, not like a "poster boy for a political cause", as he describes it. To Roger, the music and liturgy of the Latin Mass are not as rousing and sublime as the Anglican liturgy, but he's happy to be there nevertheless.

He explains that he left the Catholic Church because he felt that a bishop had told him he was irrelevant, and the liturgy told him he was a prude. He came back because he believes that the Church finds his holiness most relevant and his prudishness most welcome.

It's a grievous matter that Roger felt unaccepted by his bishop. We all want to be loved and accepted for who we are, especially by the shepherd to whose flock we belong. However, homosexuality is a sensitive and sometimes volatile subject and cannot always be addressed up-front and in the moment. There's always the careful balance between offering pastoral care and inciting antagonism.

It may have been better if Roger called the bishop and requested a meeting, because it appears that he caught the bishop off-guard at a public event.

Beyond doubt, the *Catechism* tells us that men and women with homosexual tendencies must be accepted with respect, compassion, and sensitivity, and that we should avoid every sign of unjust discrimination toward them. Just as everyone else, homosexuals are called to fulfill God's will in their lives and, if they are Christians, to unite the sufferings they experience as a result of their sexual orientation to the sacrifice of the Lord's Cross (2358). It also states that homosexual persons are called to chastity. It encourages them to reach toward inner freedom through self-mastery and resolutely approach Christian perfection by prayer and sacramental grace (2359). While the Church opposes homosexual activity because it is contrary to natural law and therefore opposes same-sex marriage, it is not uncompassionate toward those who identify themselves as homosexual.

What does Scripture say?

Be patient, therefore, beloved, until the coming of the Lord. The farmer waits for the precious crop from the earth, being patient with it until it receives the early and the late rains. You also must be patient. Strengthen your hearts, for the coming of the Lord is near. Beloved, do not grumble against one another, so that you may not be judged. See, the Judge is standing at the doors! As an example of suffering and patience, beloved, take the prophets who spoke in the name of the Lord. Indeed we call blessed those who showed endurance. You have heard of the endurance of Job, and you have seen the purpose of the

Lord, how the Lord is compassionate and merciful.

Above all, my beloved, do not swear, either by heaven or by earth or by any other oath, but let your "Yes" be yes and your "No" be no, so that you may not fall under condemnation.

JAMES 5:7–12

What does my heart say?

- ° Have I ever been unexpectedly asked a question about a sensitive or volatile issue? How did I handle that situation?
- ° We are all called to resolutely approach Christian perfection by prayer and sacramental grace. What does that mean to me?
- ° Why does the Church seek to uphold natural law? What are the consequences when it is violated?

~~~~~~

Destined for the Priesthood

James was raised by his mother and grandmother. His father deserted the family when he discovered that James' mother was pregnant with him. As a result, James had no father figure during his formative years. His mother tried to fill that void by forming relationships with older men. Being a single parent, his mother worked two jobs and was out of the house for most of the day, so his grandmother was his primary caregiver. His mother never went to church and didn't believe in the Real Presence, so his grandmother also took charge of his Catholic religious education.

At the age of seven or eight, he began to contemplate the priestly vocation. He remembers coming home from church on Sundays and saying Mass for his stuffed animals. His grandmother did her best to foster that vocation, scraping together the money for his religious education and asking for a scholarship from the parish priest when she fell short. His grandmother's health declined in his middle school years and she was unable to accompany James to church, so he rode his bike to Sunday and daily Mass, participating as an altar server.

The pressure of being a model student who people assumed was destined for the priesthood eventually became too much for James, and he began unhealthy relationships with certain individuals. Because of his family situation, he was free to come and go as he pleased and would often be gone for long periods of time, carousing and committing small misdemeanors. His petty crimes escalated, and as a result he spent four days in a juvenile detention facility facing numerous charges. At the end of the four days, he was taken to a court hearing in handcuffs and shackles. Looking back, he realizes that those were the worst days of his life. He had been expelled from school, convicted, and sentenced to a boys' reformatory camp until he turned seventeen years old.

In what he describes as an act of God's mercy and compassion, the court offered him a plea bargain in which he could do community service to satisfy the charges. He accepted, and fulfilled his commitment through a church leadership retreat that summer. He became reacquainted with his sixth-grade teacher, a loving and understanding nun who helped guide him. She also submitted James' name as a candidate to greet the new bishop of his diocese at his installation Mass on behalf of all the diocesan youth. During the event, James had a conversation with the bishop that became a turning point in his life.

His record was expunged in his sophomore year of high school, and about that time a lady from his parish invited him on a trip to Medjugorje with her tour group. He agreed to go and set out on a pilgrimage to the apparition site, which became a catalyst in amending his life. In preparation for the trip, he had begun researching not only the apparition site, but also his Catholic faith, and his heart began to transform. He returned to Mass, received reconciliation, prayed the rosary, and read Scripture. He started thinking again about being a priest.

After his return from Medjugorje, he attended an event at a Marian pilgrimage place in his diocese. The bishop was the main celebrant; he gave a homily in which he challenged those listening to become more like the Blessed Virgin Mary and to respond generously to the call of God in their lives, wherever that call might lead. For James, this was a direct confirmation of his priestly vocation, and he made the decision to apply to the diocesan seminary.

One day during his senior year in high school, he was summoned to the office for a phone call. It was his mother, and she was calling to tell him that she needed him to come to the hospital immediately because her boyfriend had tried to kill her. James left school immediately and went to the hospital just three blocks away. For the first time in his life, he told his mother that he loved her. The crisis had started him thinking about what would happen if his mother did not survive. This experience began a new level of relationship between mother and son but, most importantly, helped James' mother embark on her own faith journey. In later reflection, James realized that God had spared his mother's life so that she could get it back on track. This trial also made his own faith stronger and deepened his conviction that he was destined for the priesthood.

He entered the seminary but soon began to doubt his decision. He questioned whether he should have turned down a full scholarship at another college. On top of that, the transition into the seminary had not been going as well as he had hoped. He found himself miserable and discontent, and by mid-semester he decided to transfer to the other college and study political science and media communications. He loved his studies, but knew deep inside that they were not truly fulfilling him. He again found himself miserable and discontent.

To squelch the discontent, he ran for political office in his hometown. He was not victorious, but he did receive 400 votes to his opponent's 830 votes—a remarkable accomplishment. Ironically, an investigation uncovered conspiracy and corruption in his opponent's affairs, forcing his opponent to resign. Disillusioned by this corruption, James realized that he would never want to seek political office again. He changed his course of study and began to focus more on communications.

That summer he attended the International Eucharistic Congress in Québec City. He met a friend of his who had joined an order of religious sisters, and she invited him to attend Eucharistic Adoration with her. He accepted, and for the first time since he had left the seminary he felt a sense of peace and surrender to God. He knew then that his only option was to return to the seminary where he now continues his studies for the priesthood.

God doesn't always create straight paths for us. Sometimes God allows us to wander around on our own volition, knowing that even the most serious mistakes can eventually give way to a greater good. The darkest tunnel can lead to the brightest light.

What does Scripture say?

"If you direct your heart rightly, you will stretch out your hands toward him. If iniquity is in your hand, put it far away, and do not let wickedness reside in your tents. Surely then you will lift up your face without blemish; you will be secure, and will not fear. You will forget your misery; you will remember it as waters that have passed away. And your life will be brighter than the noonday; its darkness will be like the morning. And you will have confidence, because there is hope; you will be protected and take your rest in safety. You will lie down, and no one will make you afraid; many will entreat your favor. But the eyes of the wicked will fail; all way of escape will be lost to them, and their hope is to breathe their last."

JOB 11:13–20

What does my heart say?

- Which people in my life have had the greatest influence on my relationship with God? How have they influenced me?
- Does my life look like a straight path or a dark tunnel? Why?
- How is it that some of the most serious mistakes can lead to a greater good? Can I see any examples of that in my own life?

〰〰〰

No Accident

Nicole's friend and role model committed suicide a few weeks before she began her sophomore year at a Catholic college. The two girls would have been neighbors in the residence hall, and walking past the door of the room her friend would have occupied was traumatic for Nicole. The college was lacking in orthodox doctrinal teaching. Nicole had no Catholic community to lean on, and she was falling into sin. She rejected God, stopped attending Mass and reconciliation, and was constantly plagued by temptations.

A new student moved into the next room, and she and Nicole became close friends. They persuaded each other to commit mortal sin and regularly drove downtown together to spend nights at the homes of strangers chugging alcoholic beverages, playing beer pong, and smoking cigarettes and marijuana. The more Nicole participated, the more obsessive it became. All she wanted to do was attend more and more parties. The compulsion consumed her.

At the same time, she was working at an upscale clothing store that advertised sex and employed a photographer who used to be in the pornography industry. Nicole worked as a "brand representative" or model, and her manager rated the models on a regular basis by taking pictures of them and sending them to the corporate office. There they would be judged and rated. The "top five" were considered the five most attractive associates in the company, a recognition that would eventually lead to being a poster model for the entire corporation.

Nicole enjoyed working at the store with its blaring music, overuse of fragrance, and dark lights because it made her feel as though she were better and more attractive than all the people who didn't work there. It boosted her confidence. She judged every person who walked in the front door of the store and glared down at anyone she felt wasn't attractive enough to shop there. Somewhere in the pit of her gut she hated the company, but she had worked there for three years and had become brainwashed. Before leaving for work each day, she fretted that she was too fat, too ugly, too pale, and not good enough to work there.

Her friends outside of work made comments about her negativity, and she slowly withdrew from friends and family and spent every moment she could at the store. The only thing she wanted was to be associated with that company. If she wasn't at the store, she was trying to get drunk or high in dangerous surroundings. After a while, she developed two eating disorders and feared weight gain because she could potentially lose her position as model for the company. She made selfish decisions and became infatuated with checking mirrors and scales. She weighed ninety pounds—critically underweight for her 5'4" frame. A friend suggested seeking professional help, and refused to talk to her again unless she followed through. She was afraid, lonely, and wanted to stop feeling so ugly, but she didn't know how. Her life was slowly slipping away; she was wasting it on materialism and amoral values. She replaced her diet pills and poor eating habits with cocaine and partying routines with her new model friends at the company.

An old friend recommended that she make the two-hour drive to seek advice from a mutual Catholic friend. She went, and even though she wasn't particularly interested in listening, the friend reminded her of her need for the sacraments. Furthermore, the friend convinced her to throw away all the stashes of drugs she had in her purse and made her promise that she would never take drugs again. Nicole went along with it, at the same time plotting ways in which she could gather more drugs when she got home. Before she left, her friend gave her an icon of Our Lady of Perpetual Help.

It began to snow on the way back, and after about fifteen minutes of driving on the freeway the snow started coming down in buckets. She could barely see enough to drive. She had been on the road for three hours, and the cars were still driving at about thirty miles per hour. She was keeping to the left lane, trying to stay out of traffic, when a semi truck came up behind her and passed her in the right lane. Mounds of snow fell from the roof of the truck and, along with the winter winds, completely covered her windshield. She was terrified. She could no longer make out the lines on the highway or the headlights of the other cars. Her car began to spin, spinning so fast

that it gave her the sensation of being on a roller coaster with absolutely no control. Everything went white. She thought she was dead.
She heard crashing sounds, a loud banging of metal against metal,
scraping, windows breaking, and the sounds of other cars trying to
slow down while being whipped around and around.

Finally the car stopped. She thrust open her door. She found
herself in the median. There was a man at her side saying, "Don't
worry. I am a philologist. You were just in a horrible accident. Are
you hurt?" A woman came running up, saying, "I'm a registered
nurse. Let me make sure you are okay. Do you feel pain anywhere?"
These people were at the scene so fast that Nicole was sure they were
angels. An ambulance came. Her car was towed away. Her dad arrived and picked her up. It had all happened fast: Her car had turned
around, rotating from the lane that she was driving in, spun across
the median, and onto the opposite side of the freeway going in the
other direction. It had hit another car, flown all the way back across,
and stopped. The tow-truck driver told her that, scientifically, her
car should have been hit head-on and therefore she should have been
dead. The icon of Our Lady of Perpetual Help had fallen down on
the seat next to her—the only part of the car that had not been hit.
The entire back end of the car, starting inches from the driver's seat,
was completely smashed off.

Nicole knew the accident was a wake-up call from heaven. She had
survived something that should have killed her. She's been clean since
that date, visits the gym regularly, and is working with a nutritionist
to eat healthily. She quit her job at the clothing store and disassociated from friends who steered her away from the Church. She lived
at home for a semester and transferred to another university the
next year. She found a new job and volunteers at the local Catholic
bookstore. She's made daily Mass a priority and daily devotions a

requirement. The change hasn't been easy, but she is finally at peace and has given everything over to God. She realizes that life isn't about her; it's about the cross.

What does Scripture say?

I said to myself, "Come now, I will make a test of pleasure; enjoy yourself." But again, this also was vanity. I said of laughter, "It is mad," and of pleasure, "What use is it?" I searched with my mind how to cheer my body with wine—my mind still guiding me with wisdom—and how to lay hold on folly, until I might see what was good for mortals to do under heaven during the few days of their life. I made great works; I built houses and planted vineyards for myself; I made myself gardens and parks, and planted in them all kinds of fruit trees. I made myself pools from which to water the forest of growing trees. I bought male and female slaves, and had slaves who were born in my house; I also had great possessions of herds and flocks, more than any who had been before me in Jerusalem. I also gathered for myself silver and gold and the treasure of kings and of the provinces; I got singers, both men and women, and delights of the flesh, and many concubines. So I became great and surpassed all who were before me in Jerusalem; also my wisdom remained with me. Whatever my eyes desired I did not keep from them; I kept my heart from no pleasure, for my heart found pleasure in all my toil, and this was my reward for all my toil. Then I considered all that my hands had done and the toil I had spent in doing it, and again, all was vanity and a chasing after wind, and there was nothing to be gained under the sun.

ECCLESIASTES 2:1–11

What does my heart say?

- What are my primary weaknesses? How can I identify them?
- Are there things about which I find myself obsessing?
  What are they?
- Is toil always a good thing? Why or why not?

~~~~~

Bible Study

When Courtney was thirteen, her parish priest defied the Magisterium of the Catholic Church, was excommunicated, and formed a schismatic group. The parish and its leaders openly supported women's ordination and even let a woman hold the chalice during the consecration of the Mass. They performed gay-commitment ceremonies and invited anyone to receive the Eucharist regardless of their standing in the faith.

At the time, Courtney didn't know much about Catholicism even though she had attended Catholic schools since kindergarten. Her father was a lapsed Catholic and her mother a liberal Protestant who vehemently supported the parish's defiance of Church hierarchy. In turmoil, Courtney decided that there was no absolute Truth, and she turned her back on Christianity altogether.

By the time she was a senior in high school, she realized that she wanted a more structured faith life than agnosticism provided, but she still had doubts about Christians. She began the long and arduous process of converting to Judaism. She met her husband in college, a man who had been a committed nondenominational Christian since the age of seven. He helped her rediscover her Christian faith, and she came to love Jesus. All of her friends were faithful and believing non-Catholics, and so she became a practicing evangelical Protestant. After several years, she and her husband were married by a Southern Baptist minister and things were good, but she still had some questions.

To the astonishment of her Protestant family and friends, the Bible is what brought her back to her Catholic faith. Studying Scripture from many different Christian denominational perspectives and from the perspective of Judaism forced her to face the fact that the Scriptures really could be logically interpreted by faithful God-fearing people in a myriad of conflicting and contrasting ways. She was plunged into a frenzy of questions and wrestled with God through the Word and in prayer.

In the end God revealed to her, through the Word, the only logical conclusion: That God had granted authority to the Catholic Church, which continues to be led by the Spirit today, helping it to correctly interpret and to live out God's Word. She was immediately ready to rush home to the Catholic faith, but it took a while for her husband to adjust. Two years later, she and her husband had their marriage validated by their parish priest, and she returned to full communion with the Catholic Church. They're now extremely active in their parish and enjoying every minute of it.

Looking back, Courtney is grateful for her time away from the Church. Ironically, it brought her to a saving faith in Christ and a passionate love for him and his Church. She'll be forever grateful to her Protestant brethren for leading her to the faith, and she's now passionately committed to leading others—particularly her own children—to faith in Christ within the loving guidance and true teachings of the Catholic Church.

What does Scripture say?

When a great crowd gathered and people from town after town came to him, he said in a parable: "A sower went out to sow his seed; and as he sowed, some fell on the path and was trampled on, and the birds of the air ate it up. Some fell on the rock; and as it grew up, it withered for lack of moisture. Some fell among thorns, and the thorns grew with it and choked it. Some fell into good soil, and when it grew, it produced a hundredfold." As he said this, he called out, "Let anyone with ears to hear listen!" Then his disciples asked him what this parable meant. He said, "To you it has been given to know the secrets of the kingdom of God; but to others I speak in parables, so that 'looking they may not perceive, and listening they may not understand.' Now the parable is this: The seed is the word of God. The ones on the path are those who have heard; then the devil comes and takes away the word from their hearts, so that they may not believe and be saved. The ones on the rock are those who, when they hear the word, receive it with joy. But these have no root; they believe only for a while and in a time of testing fall away. As for what fell among the thorns, these are the ones who hear; but as they go on their way, they are choked by the cares and riches and pleasures of life, and their fruit does not mature. But as for that in the good soil, these are the ones who, when they hear the word, hold it fast in an honest and good heart, and bear fruit with patient endurance."

LUKE 8:4–15

What does my heart say?

° What do I know about the Word of God?

° What more would I like to know? How can I find out?

° What kind of soil am I for the Word of God?

~~~~~~

Do Your Own Thing

Justin and Tammy didn't get married in his home parish as they had hoped. Instead, they got married in an unfamiliar parish because Justin's pastor said he didn't like the priest they'd chosen to marry them and wouldn't allow him to marry them in his church.

At the end of that year, their first baby was born, but he lived only two-and-a-half days. A member of the Armed Forces, Justin had been stationed in another state at the time of his baby's birth. He and his wife tried to make arrangements to have the baby's body flown home and to arrange to have the Funeral Mass at his home parish. Once again, the pastor refused them. He claimed that they could not have a Funeral Mass because the baby was too young. Justin's mother talked to the pastor twice, trying to convince him to allow the Mass, and was refused both times. Justin threatened to find a non-Catholic church that would hold the service, and his father went to talk to the pastor again. Justin doesn't know what his dad said, but somehow he convinced the pastor to agree.

Before this, Justin and his wife had already been drifting away from the Catholic Church; afterward, it became quite easy. Justin found things to do on Sunday mornings other than attend Mass. He became caught up in the "do your own thing" trend, bought into the relativity of truth philosophy, and saw God as a distant being who had no effect on his life. This attitude persisted for twenty-five years.

There were consequences. Justin and Tammy divorced after eighteen years of marriage. He walked away from her and their three children (one of whom is severely brain damaged) and sought his own happiness. His marriage was followed by two relationships with women who had problems of their own. After eight years of emotional turmoil, he slowly went from being sad, to being depressed, and, on Father's Day of that year, descended into despair. All of his failures rested squarely on his shoulders, and he was numb with emotional pain.

Living temporarily on the East Coast for business purposes in a one-bedroom apartment, he spent the day watching the clock and waiting to go back to bed, the only way he could escape. Around five o'clock PM, he looked at a photograph of his deceased parents and spontaneously prayed, "I can't do this anymore. I need some help." He didn't really expect his prayer to be answered and went to bed shortly thereafter.

The next morning he woke up and immediately sensed that something was different. He started the coffee and wondered what was going on inside him. After some consideration, he was able to name it. It was peace. His heart knew that this was a gift from God and the answer to his prayer from the night before. He also heard a voice in his heart that said, "Do the right thing today and I'll take care of tomorrow."

Months passed, and he strived to live by the instructions that have been given to him. He didn't go to church, but the focus of his life changed from himself to the God who had pulled him from that dark abyss. But he had a lot of emotional healing to do, and he spent the first few months thinking about this loving God, praying the simplest of prayers, and cherishing his newfound peace.

Sometime later, his ex-wife had an emotional breakdown, and she called him for help. He raced over, looked her in the eye, and understood she was in trouble. He knew at that moment that he would be her friend and would help her get through this. She sought counseling and, helped by antidepressant drugs, she made slow progress.

On the day before Thanksgiving, during one of her bouts of uncontrollable crying, she prayed a prayer similar to Justin's and the next morning woke up experiencing the same peace and love that he had. She ended counseling and medications. A few months later, Justin moved back to his hometown and rented an apartment near his ex-wife's house. His ex-wife and her twin sister joined an Assemblies of God church, the same one his daughter attended. He woke up one morning and knew he had to go with them and continued doing so for the next ten years. During that time, he and his ex-wife remarried.

One Sunday, the pastor at the Assemblies of God church said that all Catholics were going to hell because they were not born-again. Upset, Justin left and knew he would never return. Without a church, he waited months for God to give him some direction. He missed going to church and was getting desperate. Browsing the Internet one day, he came upon the Web site for a Marian pilgrimage place and saw that he could light an electronic vigil candle and submit a prayer to Mary. He asked Mary, "Where do I belong?" This took place at the time of Pope John Paul II's death, and curiosity urged Justin to learn more about his life. He started channel surfing and found a segment by Father John Corapi about Matthew 16:17–20. Although he had read that passage many times before, he now understood that Christ named Peter the head of the Catholic Church and gave him unique authority. He started hearing about the early church Fathers and learned that the early church was essentially the same as the Catholic Church today.

This put Justin in a critical position. He loved the worship services at the Assemblies of God church. He loved singing the songs they sung. But Truth was leading him back to the Catholic Church, and he was being forced to make a decision. That summer he traveled to the Marian pilgrimage place he had found on the Internet, went to reconciliation, attended Mass, and spent half the day there giving thanks to God.

What does Scripture say?

But we have this treasure in clay jars, so that it may be made clear that this extraordinary power belongs to God and does not come from us.

We are afflicted in every way, but not crushed; perplexed, but not driven to despair; persecuted, but not forsaken; struck down, but not destroyed; always carrying in the body the death of Jesus, so that the life of Jesus may also be made visible in our bodies. For while we live, we are always being given up to death for Jesus' sake, so that the life of Jesus may be made visible in our mortal flesh. So death is at work in us, but life in you. But just as we have the same spirit of faith that is in accordance with scripture—"I believed, and so I spoke" —we also believe, and so we speak, because we know that the one who raised the Lord Jesus will raise us also with Jesus, and will bring us with you into his presence. Yes, everything is for your sake, so that grace, as it extends to more and more people, may increase thanksgiving, to the glory of God.

2 CORINTHIANS 4:7–15

What does my heart say?

- Have I ever had to say "no" to a request and been unable to help the other person understand my reasons for doing so? What was that like?
- Have I or anyone close to me ever experienced despair? When? What was it like?
- What does it mean that, while we live, we are always being "given up to death for Jesus' sake"?

∿∿∿∿

Divinely Engineered

Melanie isn't sure how she became estranged from her Catholic faith, but she can point to contributing factors. For one, she was poorly catechized. There were plenty of things that she didn't understand, but they were more or less swept under the rug. Though her family considered themselves "good Catholics" and Sunday Mass was a priority, God was not a part of their everyday lives. Melanie can count on one hand the number of times she received reconciliation as a child, and the Eucharist was merely something that marked the end of Mass.

During her college years, Melanie continued to attend Mass regularly, more out of habit than devotion. The two switches were tripped, as she describes it. The first was her decision to pursue a well-paying engineering career regardless of consequence. The second switch tripped when she was dragged to a Protestant Bible study by the same college friend with whom she often attended daily Mass. The Protestant students refuted key Catholic doctrines such as those regarding the Blessed Virgin Mary, the Eucharist, and reconciliation. She had no idea how to rebut their refutations. If that wasn't bad enough, it became obvious that everyone in the group was expected to give testimony. She avoided doing so, and made her exit from the group after two more sessions. But the damage had been done; doubts about her Catholic faith crept in. After college, a number of life-changing events occurred. Melanie began her career in engineering, and her mother began a long battle with cancer that eventually led to her death. Within two years, Melanie married a coworker and began attending law school at night while continuing to work full time. She was angry with God for taking her mother away, and her attendance at Mass became less regular. She was just too busy to fit it in.

She finished law school and took a job as an attorney. In the process, she adopted an attitude of quiet defiance toward the Church that became more hostile in the wake of the sex-abuse scandals. She felt the Church had no right to give her rules for her life, and that it was arrogant to think that only Catholics held the Truth. If she did go to Mass, she remained silent during the profession of faith and skipped Communion. She says her spiritual maturity at that point was that of a child: It had stagnated during years of neglect and eventually turned to outright callousness. She lived a paradox, willingly submitting to the authority of her employer, her professors, law enforcement, and so on while at the same time resenting the authority of the Church.

Melanie says it all boils down to a lack of vigilance. She had the ability to do something about her doubts yet avoided addressing them. She thinks she knew deep down that if she went seeking the answers to the questions that had been raised, God would want more of her than she was willing to give, and that would have messed up all of her carefully made plans. She was kept away from the Church by her preoccupation with her career and her materialistic goals. Her life revolved around her work.

She and her husband Ron bought a house and began a steady stream of home improvements. Ron also was Catholic, and from time to time they made a weak effort to get back on track with their faith but were never successful. They put off having children because Melanie didn't want to seem anything but serious about her career. There was even a period of time when she thought she might not want children at all. They finally had their first child ten years into their marriage.

The question of baptism arose. Although Melanie had lapsed in her own Catholic faith, she did not want to bring her son up with no faith at all, and this haunted her. There were some uncomfortable moments when Melanie and her husband were uncertain about whether the godparents would meet the Church's requirements, and it became painfully obvious at the ceremony itself that Melanie's nieces and nephews were not receiving religious education. Her most prominent memory of that day was of being focused on appearances rather than the sacrament. She had simply gone through the motions.

She took a six-month leave of absence from work to care for her son and thoroughly enjoyed it. The time away from a professional environment opened her heart a little bit. Motherhood allowed her to experience genuine adult femininity, not in a perfume and high heels way, but in an emotional, nurturing way. She had been forging a path through a man's world for more than ten years, playing by a set of masculine rules for behavior that had, she thinks, done some damage. Time away gave her a chance to heal, but she still had her eyes on the corporate ladder.

Their second son was born two years later, and she again took a leave of absence to care for him. Upon returning to work, she accepted a promotion to a higher-level management position. A year into it she realized that, as much as she liked her job, it was consuming too much of her time and too much of herself. She was working nine or more hours in the office each day and another few hours late at night. She was also beginning to appreciate the difference between mothers and fathers and husbands and wives, and it dawned on her that they are naturally wired differently, with different abilities and susceptibilities. She realized that because of this, she and her husband must work together as a team, that running a household is not a relay race, and children are not batons. She concluded that she had to step back, give up her management position, and accept a part-time assignment.

That was one of the best decisions she ever made in her life, but it didn't come without a good deal of pain and anger—pain at having to step back from the career she had valued highly and would be unlikely to regain; anger because she felt she'd been duped by the culture into believing that she could have it all.

It didn't take long for her to be comfortable and happy with the decision. She was more present with her family. Her role at work was limited but still important, and she had a great boss. She and her husband began attending Mass here and there, and were developing a social life. One day at a barbecue, she was comparing notes with some friends from work who had moved into the same town. They were discussing the local parish and Mass attendance. Melanie made a flippant remark about her friend being "so good" because she went to Mass every week. She made excuses for her own spotty attendance, citing lack of time. Her girlfriend looked her in the eye and said matter-of-factly that if she wanted to go to Mass she had to make it a priority.

Things began happening all at once. At the same time that Melanie's oldest son entered second grade, she'd become restless and dissatisfied with her work. She felt trapped and was contemplating leaving the company. Not only that, she was beginning to question the value of work on a more basic level. She began to feel guilty about spending all her time and energy trying to achieve her own selfish goals and failing to direct some of her time and energy toward helping the less fortunate. She discovered Peggy Noonan's book, *John Paul II the Great: Remembering a Spiritual Father*, and listened to it on CD several times. She saw her Catholic faith in a new light. In the back of her mind she kept hearing the question, "How could I have missed all of this?" She began to think that perhaps God was calling her to do something different with her life, although she had no idea what that was. She began looking around at the local nonprofit organizations trying to find where she belonged. Question after question popped up, and this time she felt compelled to find answers, not just silence them.

She began attending both Sunday and daily Mass simply because she felt she needed to be there. Her oldest son began preparation for the sacrament of reconciliation, and she had to ask herself how she could expect her son to receive the sacrament when she did not do so herself. She began to feel real repentance and regretted her years of spiritual neglect. As hard as it was, she received reconciliation, her first real "yes" to God in a very long time. In the midst of all this, she received a new work assignment—one that offered the best possible scenario. But it was too little, too late. After a few months, she quit her job and worked only on a consulting basis. She started volunteering for nonprofits and attending more church functions. She met a good priest who she trusted and with whom she could connect, and he became her spiritual director.

She still can't see clearly where God is leading her, and sometimes her imagination gets the better of her and she becomes impatient to figure it out. The one thing she can see clearly is that God is pulling her closer, and she knows now that she's on her way home.

What does Scripture say?

I therefore, the prisoner in the Lord, beg you to lead a life worthy of the calling to which you have been called, with all humility and gentleness, with patience, bearing with one another in love, making every effort to maintain the unity of the Spirit in the bond of peace. There is one body and one Spirit, just as you were called to the one hope of your calling, one Lord, one faith, one baptism, one God and Father of all, who is above all and through all and in all. But each of us was given grace according to the measure of Christ's gift. Therefore it is said, "When he ascended on high he made captivity itself a captive; he gave gifts to his people." The gifts he gave were that some would be apostles, some prophets, some evangelists, some pastors and teachers, to equip the saints for the work of ministry, for building up the body of Christ, until all of us come to the unity of the faith and of the knowledge of the Son of God, to maturity, to the measure of the full stature of Christ. We must no longer be children, tossed to and fro and blown about by every wind of doctrine, by people's trickery, by their craftiness in deceitful scheming. But speaking the truth in love, we must grow up in every way into him who is the head, into Christ, from whom the whole body, joined and knit together by every ligament with which it is equipped, as each part is working properly, promotes the body's growth in building itself up in love.

EPHESIANS 4:1–8, 11–16

What does my heart say?

- Have I ever had a feeling that something is about to happen, but couldn't really put my finger on it? When? What was that like?
- Have I ever had the feeling that God was trying to show me something? When? How did I respond?
- God has given everyone unique gifts. What are mine? How am I using them? How would I like to be using them?

Skewed Relationship

For years, Janine carried the burden of the sexual abuse she suffered from ages twelve to eighteen. She blamed herself for this great sin. One night, when she was about thirty-five years old, she was watching television and a documentary called Sins of the Father came on. It was about a priest who had sexually abused others. The show's producer interviewed an FBI agent, and the agent was talking about how difficult sexual abuse in general is for girls, how confusing it can be, because it is a male-female relationship and girls are conditioned to be submissive to men. In a flash, she knew what had happened to her. She began to wail uncontrollably; the pain and confusion were almost more than she could bear.

She spent the first forty-seven years of her life unable to accept God's tremendous love. Because of this, her relationship with God was skewed. In an effort to heal from her past experiences, she joined Alcoholics Anonymous. One night at a meeting someone asked her, "If you believe so strongly in a God, where was God when all these things happened to you?" Her life had been abuse after abuse, from the time she was a child. She left the meeting in tears—she had never considered that question before. More frightened than ever, she pleaded with God and asked, "Where were you?"

It seemed to Janine that God replied as audibly as she had spoken a moment before. She heard a voice say, "I gave men free will and they sin, but I will always be with you." She isn't sure where the voice came from, but her heart knew that it was somehow a message from God. It sustained her and helped her to begin working through her troubles. From the time she was very little, she had always had an insatiable need to understand, but allowing herself to feel, to face the abuse, was often too painful. As time went on, she replaced her need to know with faith in God. It was a slow process.

She had to separate the Church from the institution. For her, that meant that she did not have to agree with all the rules, but she did have to respect and follow them. She had to stop looking out at all the pain and look into a God who is within her and shares with her all that she experienced. She had to learn that God does not cause our suffering, but will find a way to use it for God's greater plan. She would never want to relive what she's been through, but she would never change it either, because it has now become a source of strength for her. She had to understand that the Church is made up of both sinners and saints, and that there would continue to be times of hurt and pain. But the abuse of the past would no longer be her future.

Janine had been gone from the Church for seven years; now it was time to begin the journey back. She found a parish in which she felt needed and accepted, and where she could freely use her gifts. She's grown in ways that she never would have thought possible and has found new purpose and meaning in life. The greatest gift is knowing that all is good—every challenge, every joy, every sorrow, and every tear—that within this community of faith she's never alone. Her life will continue to grow into all that God finds possible for her. God has instilled in her the desire to take responsibility for her Catholic faith and to live it in such a way that she can be an example of God's love for others.

What does Scripture say?

Beloved, let us love one another, because love is from God; everyone who loves is born of God and knows God. Whoever does not love does not know God, for God is love. God's love was revealed among us in this way: God sent his only Son into the world so that we might live through him. In this is love, not that we loved God but that he loved us and sent his Son to be the atoning sacrifice for our sins. Beloved, since God loved us so much, we also ought to love one another. No one has ever seen God; if we love one another, God lives in us, and his love is perfected in us. By this we know that we abide in him and he in us, because he has given us of his Spirit.

And we have seen and do testify that the Father has sent his Son as the Savior of the world. God abides in those who confess that Jesus is the Son of God, and they abide in God. So we have known and believe the love that God has for us. God is love, and those who abide in love abide in God, and God abides in them. Love has been perfected among us in this: that we may have boldness on the day of judgment, because as he is, so are we in this world. There is no fear in love, but perfect love casts out fear; for fear has to do with punishment, and whoever fears has not reached perfection in love. We love because he first loved us.

1 JOHN 4:7–19

What does my heart say?

- ° Am I able to accept God's love? Why or why not?
- ° Do I tend to hold an entire group responsible for the actions of a single member? In families...the workplace...government... the Church?
- ° What does "everyone who loves is born of God and knows God" mean?

vvvvvvvv

From Porn Addiction to God Addiction

Bob's entire family fell away from the Church after his parents divorced. At that time, he was thirteen years old, and had received the sacrament of confirmation. He figured that he was no longer required to attend religious education classes or church liturgies, and, since there was no one around to tell him that he had to, he just stopped going.

He became involved in drugs and alcohol, not understanding the damage he was doing to himself. He continued on this path for the next twenty years, addicted to marijuana and pornography. Partying was a priority. Strangely, he didn't really enjoy it, but he kept it up anyway because his friends did. He hated his job, was very lonely and miserable, and his life seemed meaningless.

At the age of thirty-one, he suffered an injury at work that left him with a herniated disc that required surgery. There was a remote possibility that he could be paralyzed from the neck down if something went wrong during the operation. He was scared and asked his mother to pray for him. The pain before surgery was excruciating; the pain afterward was even worse. He was off work for six months.

He managed to work for the next six months, in constant pain, and he considered requesting a disability leave. Christmas was coming; he'd see how things were after the holiday break. About this time, his twin brother converted to the Seventh Day Adventist Church, and his wife gave Bob a Bible for Christmas. He wasn't much interested in it, but placed it on top of his stereo speaker box so that people who came to visit him would think he was religious. He cleaned up his entertainment center one day and inadvertently laid some of his pornographic videotapes on top of the Bible. When he looked away, he heard a crash; the tapes had fallen off the Bible and onto the floor.

That January he returned to work and, after a week or so, noticed that for the most part his neck pain was gone. He started to think about this, and it occurred to him that ever since the Bible had been given to him he had experienced very little pain in his neck. He wondered if perhaps he should start reading the Bible but didn't know where to start. He opened the book to the Gospel of Matthew, choosing it simply because it was the first book in the New Testament. But he was confused. He couldn't understand many of the sayings, especially ones like "It is easier for a camel to go through the eye of a needle than for someone who is rich to enter the kingdom of God" (Matthew 19:24). He knew he needed some instruction but didn't like the Scriptural interpretations offered by his brother's church. Where could he go?

One night he had a dream. In his dream, his mother was poor and in debt to a Mafia gangster. He went to the mob guy's mansion and entered a dark room where there was a man wearing a mask. He told the guy that his mother was poor and had no money, and that he would pay her debt whatever the amount. The man then removed his mask and smiled. He felt the debt was forgiven, but he really didn't understand how, since he had given him no money. Then he woke up. He figured that it had been his subconscious telling him that it was time to visit his mother because he had not seen her in a long time. Perhaps he would also give her some money. He made plans to visit the following Saturday. He stopped at the bank to cash his paycheck. When he came home, he decided that he would call her right after he swept and mopped the kitchen floor. While he was sweeping, the phone rang. It was his mother. They talked, and she invited him to go to church with her the following Wednesday. Surprisingly, he agreed.

That was Ash Wednesday. The priest processed to the sanctuary and started the prayers of the Mass, and as he did so he looked up and smiled at Bob. Bob was shocked—the priest looked exactly like the man in his dream! He had never seen this priest before in his life. After Mass, Bob and his mother returned to the house, and he gave her some money. The message of the dream had gotten through to him. He began going to Mass with his mother every Sunday, and since then his faith has grown by leaps and bounds. He's given up his old lifestyle and returned to the Catholic Church with gusto. He attends Mass daily, prays constantly, does his best to walk with Jesus and Mary in every thought and action he performs, and lives in the hope of eternity.

What does Scripture say?

Now after they had left, an angel of the Lord appeared to Joseph in a dream and said, "Get up, take the child and his mother, and flee to Egypt, and remain there until I tell you; for Herod is about to search for the child, to destroy him." Then Joseph got up, took the child and his mother by night, and went to Egypt, and remained there until the death of Herod. This was to fulfill what had been spoken by the Lord through the prophet, "Out of Egypt I have called my son."

When Herod died, an angel of the Lord suddenly appeared in a dream to Joseph in Egypt and said, "Get up, take the child and his mother, and go to the land of Israel, for those who were seeking the child's life are dead." Then Joseph got up, took the child and his mother, and went to the land of Israel. But when he heard that Archelaus was ruling over Judea in place of his father Herod, he was afraid to go there. And after being warned in a dream, he went away to the district of Galilee. There he made his home in a town called Nazareth, so that what had been spoken through the prophets might be fulfilled, "He will be called a Nazorean."

MATTHEW 2:13–15, 19–23

What does my heart say?

- Have I ever had a dream that seemed to hold a particular message for me? What was it?
- As far as I can tell, was it a message from God or my own conscience working in the night? How did I know?
- Why did God give a message to Joseph in a dream? Why not some other way?

~~~~~~

The First Stone

Sophia left the Church because she wanted to sin. She wanted to live without regard for consequences. Although she was married and had two young children, she chose to have an affair with another married person, and the Church was in her way. There was no point in confessing her sin because she was not sorry for it at the time.

Once she'd made her decision to leave the Church, she had to communicate it to her husband, Carl. She chose a Sunday morning when they were preparing to go to Mass, and the children were being difficult. She simply refused to go that morning because it was too hard to get both children dressed and ready. Carl thought that she meant only that one Sunday, but she meant all of them. That was the last Sunday any of them went to church.

At first, she was relieved not to have to think about or talk to anyone about her sin. It was just an affair, and she had no intention of staying away from the Church long term. As the months passed, however, she fell deeply in love with her extramarital partner, Randy. She knew she could not go back to the Church unless she gave him up, and she was unwilling to do that.

Since her children were young, she had little concern about their knowledge of God or the Church. She made meager attempts here and there, one time trying to register her children for Vacation Bible School at a Methodist Church. The person handling registration asked which church Sophia's family attended. When she responded that they didn't attend any church, the person said there was little point in educating the children about the Bible if the parents didn't attend church themselves. Sophia was furious and hung up on her.

She dabbled in the Mormon Church, scanning the Book of Mormon and visiting with Mormon missionaries. But when the missionaries suggested that she remove a print of the Madonna and Child that she had hanging on the wall, she became resentful and ended her association with them, too. It was no great loss, as she had difficulty accepting their teachings anyway. She continued to attend Catholic weddings and funerals but refused to kneel during any of the Masses. She was proving to herself what a jerk she had become.

Sophia's mother tried relentlessly to bring her back to the Catholic Church, but the more she tried the more hostile Sophia became. Her mother died knowing that her daughter was still distanced from the Church. As an only child, it was Sophia's responsibility to arrange the funeral, which was in a Catholic church. She was very cold to the priest and let him know that she was only following through on her mother's request. On the day of the funeral, Sophia could barely stop herself from being moved by the hymns and prayers of the Mass. Her children were grieving over the loss of their grandma but because she had never instilled the faith in them, she had no way to comfort them.

A series of life changes followed. Sophia switched careers and accepted a position in a Catholic healthcare facility. The kindness and devotion of the religious sisters who owned the system made a lasting impression on her. She was given opportunities to do works of mercy outside of the workplace, and this added a new facet to her life. She divorced Carl and married Randy six months later, breaking the hearts of those who cared about her, including her children's. Randy died nine months later, and she was devastated. The religious sisters and other staff members were so comforting and supportive that she almost considered going back to the Church. Almost.

One Saturday night four years later, she was ironing and watching television. She was depressed, fretting over finances, afraid of being alone, and worrying that there would never be anyone to love her. She uttered a prayer of desperation, telling God that if God ever wanted her to be happy again, God would need to send someone her way.

The following Monday the well inspector showed up at her door. She was refinancing her home, and the well inspection was part of the deal. Brad seemed compassionate and understanding. His wife had died from a terrible disease, and he knew what it was like to be alone. Sophia and Brad began a relationship and soon decided to get married. He was Lutheran and wanted to get married in his Church; even though Sophia was no longer a practicing Catholic, she wanted to get married in hers. However, since her conviction lacked strength, she eventually gave in, and she and Brad were married in the Lutheran Church. Brad, whom she called her "gift from God," died four years later of Lou Gehrig's disease.

The following summer, a pair of Jehovah's Witnesses visited Sophia at her home. She was tired and sad, and knew they'd come merely to proselytize, but she spoke with them anyway. For reasons Sophia still doesn't understand, she completely lost control, broke down crying, and told the two women about Brad. They followed up with more visits, and eventually she had to tell them not to come back as she wasn't willing to convert to their faith. Something spiritual was growing inside her.

Brad's friend, also a Lutheran, volunteered to help Sophia with her yard equipment and in the process engaged her in interesting philosophical conversations. Simon had attended a Catholic university and greatly appreciated the Jesuits and their teachings. He offered to escort her to Mass, and she accepted because she didn't want to offend him. They attended Mass together frequently for over a year. Neither of them ever received Communion, which embarrassed Sophia; she wondered if perhaps she could go back to the Church. She started to have more enthusiasm for the Mass and went on her own.

The church she was attending was staffed by an order of monks, and she began to consider the possibility of seeking spiritual direction and reconciliation. She had reservations and worried about what the monk might think of her when he heard about the way she had lived and the sins she had committed, but she knew that receiving the sacrament was the only way for her to reenter the Church. She made an appointment for a private confession with one of the monks who had seemed like a particularly compassionate person.

The morning of her confession, she had cold feet. She wanted to just turn around and forget the whole idea, but she forced herself to go nonetheless. For once in her life, she knew she was making the right decision.

What does Scripture say?

Early in the morning he came again to the temple. All the people came to him and he sat down and began to teach them. The scribes and the Pharisees brought a woman who had been caught in adultery; and making her stand before all of them, they said to him, "Teacher, this woman was caught in the very act of committing adultery. Now in the law Moses commanded us to stone such women. Now what do you say?" They said this to test him, so that they might have some charge to bring against him. Jesus bent down and wrote with his finger on the ground. When they kept on questioning him, he straightened up and said to them, "Let anyone among you who is without sin be the first to throw a stone at her." And once again he bent down and wrote on the ground. When they heard it, they went away, one by one, beginning with the elders; and Jesus was left alone with the woman standing before him. Jesus straightened up and said to her, "Woman, where are they? Has no one condemned you?" She said, "No one, sir." And Jesus said, "Neither do I condemn you. Go your way, and from now on do not sin again."

JOHN 8:2–11

What does my heart say?

- ° Do I have any sins that I fear are too great to forgive? Do I have smaller ones that are too embarrassing to admit? Why do I feel this way?
- ° If I could confess them right here and now, what would I say?
- ° Why did the people in the Scripture story drop their stones and walk away?

3
Coming
Back

My dad loved to go for long, relaxing drives in the country. On Sunday afternoons, he'd pile us kids into our old International Harvester Suburban, and we'd take off for hours and hours. Of course, those were the days when gas was relatively cheap. Even if it hadn't been, I doubt Dad would have changed his ways much.

He'd play a game with us. He'd drive way out to who-knows-where, meandering down this or that highway, curving, turning, and driving, driving, driving. Then when he figured he'd gotten us out far enough, he'd appoint one of us kids as navigator and make us find our way home. He wouldn't give us a clue—wherever we said to turn, he turned. Wherever we said to backtrack, he backtracked. He let us lead. The only times he ever intervened was when we'd gotten hopelessly lost, but then only after we'd struggled for a good long while.

Because of this, I have an uncanny sense of direction. I can find my way just about anywhere and back and rarely get lost. On the few occasions I have gotten lost, it's been because I somehow lost my bearing. Without being able to tell north from south or east from west, I'm sunk. I don't get lost often, but when I do get lost, I really get lost.

It's the same way with the Church. Those of us who have lost our bearing can no longer tell north from south or east from west. Without a sense of direction—our sense of Truth—we can get lost. And when we do get lost, we really get lost.

The stories in this chapter relate the journeys of those who have gotten lost—some of them really lost—and found their way back home to the Catholic Church.

~~~~~

By the Bootstraps

Parental support is everything when you're a young adult starting out on your own. Kelly knows this, not because she had it, but because she didn't. A naïve yet energetic girl from a small, Midwestern town, she dared to attend college in New York City, a decision for which she was relentlessly criticized by her parents.

Once in New York, she was shell-shocked. Everything was extremely different—culture, workplace, school, and people. Without parental support, she felt as though she had been thrown into the torrent and was expected to tread water. Her parents not only condemned her decision, they also refused her any financial or material assistance. She was completely alone with no one to turn to for help. She'd been raised Catholic, but had no real relationship with God, and the thought of seeking solace in her Catholic faith never even crossed her mind.

Determined and self-sufficient, Kelly resolved to pull herself up by her bootstraps and fend for herself, not an easy thing to do in a city that can be as hostile as New York. She ended up going from one bad job to another, artificially inflating her own ego to keep herself going, and becoming involved in detrimental relationships. She had no support system and felt as though she were simply twisting in the wind.

Desperate for a way to keep from being blown completely off course, she went to a bookstore and searched through the self-help section. She didn't want any books with religious content; she knew that if she turned to Christ he would make her work. She'd suffered emotional abuse throughout her childhood, something she wasn't ready to face at this point in time. She picked out a couple of books, took them home, and began to read them. After that, she frequented the self-help section a lot. Her resistance to anything religious, especially the Catholic Church, continued.

One day a book by Emmet Fox caught her eye. Fox wrote and lectured extensively on the religious meaning of life, and although she still wasn't interested in organized religion, she was interested in finding some meaning in her life. Kelly took the book home, read it, and found it to be quite helpful. Surprisingly, she found Fox's observations on the Bible and their practical applications to be lacking the sinister intent she had expected. She kept on reading self-help books, focusing more and more on Fox's works.

On her next trip to the bookstore, she couldn't find the Fox title that she was looking for even though the computer listed it as being in stock. She really wanted that book, so she decided to try something truly outrageous. She prayed. She said, "Lord, if you want to help me, if you want me to find the book by Emmet Fox, then let me find it." At that moment a store employee entered the aisle. The expression on his face made it clear that he had entered accidentally and was about to turn around when Brenda caught his attention and asked him to help her find the book. Two seconds later the book was in her hands, and she was headed for the checkout.

The bookstore experience started a chain reaction and soon Kelly found herself going into a church and simply sitting in the back pew to rest and be at peace. In the meantime, she began having financial difficulty—her job didn't pay much, and she couldn't make the rent. Embarrassingly, she received an eviction notice but could do nothing about it because she was broke. She knew she was in trouble and began to pray more frequently. She received a letter from a lawyer; it scared her, but she couldn't tell anyone about it. She prayed harder. She couldn't sleep, and she persistently felt like she had to vomit. She finally called a trusted coworker and asked her advice. The coworker suggested that she call her boss, a real estate developer. She immediately felt a release inside her, made the call, and had the money in her hands within a couple of hours. Her boss had loaned her the money interest free, handling the situation with charity and tact.

Kelly's dilemma replayed itself a couple of months later, and she was mortified. She knelt by the side of her bed and prayed frantically. Then a thought came into her head that she knew wasn't her own. It urged her to call her aunt. She did, and her aunt wired the money to her immediately. After that, Kelly failed to make the rent a third time and was summoned to court. She was absolutely terrified; she didn't know what to expect. The attorney—a substitute for the one originally scheduled to handle her case—was kind, understanding, and gently helped her through the process. She began to believe that angels could take the form of humans.

On the day of her hearing, she woke up frightened and uncertain. It was a struggle to get herself out the door and on the subway toward City Hall, but somehow she managed. An elderly woman on the subway caught her attention. She had an uncanny resemblance to Kelly's grandmother, the only person in her family with whom she had formed an attachment. She couldn't stop staring at the woman.

Looking at her brought back wonderful memories of better times and gave Kelly an inexplicable feeling of calm and assurance. It didn't solve her financial problems, but it put her in touch with a part of herself that had not been awakened for a very long time.

That was the beginning of Kelly's return to the Catholic Church. She started noticing how God was leading her in little ways. She bought an angel necklace and wore it as a reminder of the angels in human form that God had sent to help her in difficult times. She found a Bible and some Catholic books and started reading them. She prayed several times a day, moved to a new apartment, began attending Mass and receiving reconciliation regularly at the Catholic church two blocks away, and added a number of devotions to her daily routine.

Kelly describes her life like two pieces that look like they shouldn't even be in the same puzzle and yet fit perfectly together. She knows God is leading her now. She has no idea where God's leading her, but she's ready to follow.

What does Scripture say?

To you, O Lord, I lift up my soul.

O my God, in you I trust; do not let me be put to shame; do not let my enemies exult over me.

Do not let those who wait for you be put to shame; let them be ashamed who are wantonly treacherous.

Make me to know your ways, O Lord; teach me your paths.

Lead me in your truth, and teach me, for you are the God of my salvation; for you I wait all day long.

Be mindful of your mercy, O Lord, and of your steadfast love, for they have been from of old.

Do not remember the sins of my youth or my

transgressions; according to your steadfast love
remember me, for your goodness' sake, O Lord!
Good and upright is the Lord; therefore he instructs sinners
in the way.
He leads the humble in what is right, and teaches the
humble his way.
All the paths of the Lord are steadfast love and faithfulness,
for those who keep his covenant and his decrees

PSALM 25:1–10

What does my heart say?

- On whom do I depend in my life?
  What does my support system look like?
- If I consider myself self-sufficient, by what means
  do I keep myself going?
- Have I ever been in a seemingly impossible situation
  that was inexplicably resolved? What was it?

Letters From Prison

Jayden still feels like an outcast from the Church even though he's
returned to his Catholic faith. He is serving time in a state correctional institution and is sharing his story because he believes that if
even one person returns to the faith because of it, it will have been
worth everything he went through.

He had several reasons for leaving the Catholic Church, the primary one being that his parish priest repeatedly raped and molested
him until he was about ten years old. Then his family moved to a new

parish, where his Catholic Youth Organization counselor sexually abused him from ages eleven to nineteen.

He received the sacrament of confirmation at age twelve, and after that the abuse he had experienced through his priest and youth-group counselor tormented him. His father had taught him to seek the help of a priest anytime he was in trouble, and that all priests were to be highly respected and obeyed. So he went to another priest and told him about the abuse. The priest virtually scared him into silence, silence that he kept until he was forty years old. He never told anyone about the rapes and molestations that he had endured as a boy. Until he was arrested, that is.

He had become a molester himself. He still believed in God, but thought God was expecting far too much from him. From age thirteen, he ran from God, his Church, his Catholic faith, and himself. From that time forward, he felt as though a part of himself was missing.

The abuse caused him to grow up fast and to believe that he was a bad person. If he weren't a bad person, he rationalized, the second priest would have helped him. He went through life believing he had been chosen to feel the wrath of God and wondered what would have happened if he had received the help he needed or if he at least had told his parents about the abuse. He wonders if they would have helped him avoid becoming an offender himself.

Jayden kept running until he was forty-two years old. He became a workaholic, identifying himself with his work because he didn't believe that God had a place in his life. He became sexually active, especially after he learned that there were men who would pay him to use his body. This became his substitute for religion.

After he was incarcerated, he started attending the Protestant service at the correctional institution and even earned seventeen credits toward a degree with an evangelical Bible institute. The services were somewhat helpful, but he always felt afterwards as if something had been missing—almost as if he hadn't really worshiped God. He realized that he was missing the Eucharist. He missed Mass!

He went to the prison chaplain and explained how he felt, even though he wasn't sure if he could actually return to the Catholic Church. The chaplain was a Baptist minister who listened carefully, took Jayden's needs seriously, and did what he could to help him explore his Catholic faith. About that time, he saw a show on the Public Broadcasting Service station about Thomas Merton and the beauty of a contemplative faith. He read Merton's *Seven Story Mountain* and felt drawn to the idea of trying to live as a contemplative inasmuch as his situation allowed. With the help of the Catholic prison chaplain and a visiting priest, he was led to pray the Office of the Hours.

Over the next year, he wrote to several contemplative orders in hopes of studying as an oblate. His mother gave him Karl Keating's book, *Open Mind, Open Heart*. There was a list of resources in the back of the book, and Jayden happened upon the address of an order of hermitage monks. All the other orders he wrote to refused him acceptance because he'd be required to take his vows at the monastery. This order made an exception for him and allowed him to study to be an oblate. Two years later, the prison priest administered his oblate vows, and he's been striving to live as a contemplative ever since.

Due to overcrowding, some of the inmates were transferred out of state, including Jayden. The new prison was located deep in the Bible belt, and the only church service offered to the inmates was Baptist. He petitioned the chaplain for a Catholic Mass, but his request was refused. He protested, and was sent to the Chief of Security who told him, "There isn't going to be any Vatican voodoo in this institution. If you try to start a Mass, I'll put a bullet in your head and send you back to [your home state]." Jayden had let someone take his faith from him as a boy; he wasn't going to let anyone take it from him as a man. He contacted his family, and they contacted the bishop of his home diocese. A week later a priest from the nearby town came to celebrate Mass for the inmates.

Jayden's road has been long and rugged. He's finally forgiven those who harmed him, and he has forgiven himself for not having tried harder to stop the abuse. He lives his life with conviction and has pledged to never deny his faith, the Church, or himself ever again.

What does Scripture say?

Now Peter was sitting outside in the courtyard. A servant girl came to him and said, "You also were with Jesus the Galilean." But he denied it before all of them, saying, "I do not know what you are talking about." When he went out to the porch, another servant girl saw him, and she said to the bystanders, "This man was with Jesus of Nazareth." Again he denied it with an oath, "I do not know the man." After a little while the bystanders came up and said to Peter, "Certainly you are also one of them, for your accent betrays you." Then he began to curse, and he swore an oath, "I do not know the man!" At that moment the cock crowed. Then Peter remembered what Jesus had said: "Before the cock crows, you will deny me three times." And he went out and wept bitterly.

MATTHEW 26:69–75

What does my heart say?

- What caused Peter to deny that he was a follower of Jesus?
- What happened afterwards in both the short term and long term?
- What message does Peter's denial have for me? What hope does it offer me?

~~~~

Seek With All Your Heart

As a kid, Catherine liked going to church, but she never really knew what Catholics believed and didn't believe. She knew there were differences between Catholic and non-Catholic denominations, but she didn't know what they were. She had no Catholic identity. As a teen, she memorized all the prayers of the Mass but had no clue what they meant. She, like so many young people in the fallout after the Second Vatican Council, had been minimally catechized. Anything of her Catholic faith that stuck with her was associated with music. Catherine loved music and was a musician.

She dated a non-Catholic who introduced her to his Methodist pastor. His pastor was cool, and she liked him immediately. He was different from the Catholic priests she had known. She went with her boyfriend to what she calls "Jesus festivals," nondenominational gatherings for Christian youth. It was a difficult time. Confused about where she belonged, she was constantly fighting rules and morals.

The relationship with her boyfriend didn't work out. In an attempt to heal, she went to visit a friend who attended an evangelical university. She liked it, applied, and was accepted. She learned all sorts of interesting things while attending the university, and one day she just walked away from the Catholic Church without realizing what she was actually walking away from.

People of all different faiths, all different ideas, and all different practices populated the university. They held what they called communion services at which "communion" consisted of grape juice and bread, soda and taco chips, and other foods and beverages. She heard lots of preaching about lots of different things in a kind of "name it and claim it" style. On Sunday mornings, buses would line up in front of the dormitories, open the doors, and wait for the students. The buses would take them to any church they wanted to attend, and the sheer variety of choices often became the brunt of jokes. Students would pretend to be preachers, enticing others to attend "The Church of Anywhere You Want to Go."

Catherine did go anywhere she wanted to go, and more. She tried a number of different denominations, even one that promised to make her speak in tongues. It was all so confusing; she was surrounded by a lot of people with a lot of ideas, and she didn't know what she really believed. She went from one church to another, starting with Open Bible Church, which she attended with a friend for two years. Then she tried a charismatic church, then one that offered more praise and worship, and another that offered Bible study. She never really felt at home in any of them.

During her junior year, she met a young man who seemed different from all the others. They were in a class together taught by an instructor who belonged to the Pentecostal Holiness Church. The instructor had a knack for initiating debate, and she thoroughly enjoyed the exciting exchanges in class. She started dating Greg, an Episcopalian, and went to church with him. The Episcopal service was much more like the Catholic Mass than any of the other services she had attended, and she felt somewhat at home there. Consequently, she made plans to be received into the Episcopal Church. She underwent instruction, and for the first time in her life gave serious consideration to what the Catholic Church did and did not teach. She began to see the Catholic Church in a different light.

Greg, on the other hand, had been raised Episcopalian and had always believed that his calling was to be an Episcopal priest. But things in the Episcopal Church began to change in ways he couldn't accept. Together they tried the Pentecostal Episcopal Church, but in the end they weren't at home there either. About that time, they attended a lecture by apologist Patrick Madrid, and their hearts began moving in that direction. Rome was calling them. Greg, already ordained an Episcopal priest, decided to honor his commitment to the Pentecostal Episcopal Church.

They were soon married, had children, and began home schooling. The only curriculum they could find that would complement their family was Catholic. They enrolled, and Catherine began catechizing her children, herself, and eventually Greg. He had been well catechized as an Episcopal priest and didn't object to any of the teachings of the Catholic Church. What's more, the Catholic faith began to make more sense to them than any of the others they had encountered, including the Episcopal faith. They realized that there was no other option for them; they knew the Truth, and when you know the Truth there's no other place to go. They were headed home.

The following Easter, their youngest child was baptized Catholic, and the entire family was received into the Church—all ten of them. Catherine's husband turned down two salaried positions to be pastor of an Episcopal parish and is seeking ordination in the Catholic priesthood—a lengthy process requiring a dispensation from the Church. Their oldest son is studying for the Roman Catholic priesthood. Catherine has become involved in her parish's music ministry, and the whole family is active in their parish.

Catherine came back finally knowing what she had left behind—the Eucharist. To her, "transubstantiation" is no longer a scary word; it's a joyful one. She could see the hollowness of religions that relied on the Bible alone and the fallacy of those that claimed there was no Real Presence. She also discovered that other faiths do not believe that the Mass is a sacrifice and negate the existence of the communion of saints. She is convinced that if we are truly seeking with all our hearts, we'll find that the Catholic Church has the fullness of Truth, and that if we don't believe it, then we're not seeking with all our hearts.

What does Scripture say?

The Lord will scatter you among the peoples; only a few of you will be left among the nations where the Lord will lead you. There you will serve other gods made by human hands, objects of wood and stone that neither see, nor hear, nor eat, nor smell. From there you will seek the Lord your God, and you will find him if you search after him with all your heart and soul. In your distress, when all these things have happened to you in time to come, you will return to the Lord your God and heed him. Because the Lord your God is a merciful God, he will neither abandon you nor destroy you; he will not forget the covenant with your ancestors that he swore to them. For ask now about former ages, long before your own, ever since the day that God created human beings on the earth; ask from one end of heaven to the other: has anything so great as this ever happened or has its like ever been heard of? Has any people ever heard the voice of a god speaking out of a fire, as you have heard, and lived? Or has any god ever attempted to go and take a nation for himself from the midst of another nation, by trials, by signs and wonders, by war, by a mighty hand and an outstretched arm, and by terrifying displays of power, as the Lord your God did for you in Egypt before your very eyes? To you it was shown so that you would acknowledge that the Lord is God; there is no other besides him. From heaven he made you hear his voice to discipline you. On earth he showed you his great fire, while you heard his words coming out of the fire. And because he loved your ancestors, he chose their descendants after them. He brought you out of Egypt with his own presence, by his great power, driving out before you nations greater and mightier than yourselves, to bring you in, giving you their land for a possession, as it is still today. So acknowledge today and take to heart that the Lord is God in heaven above and on the earth beneath; there is no other. Keep his statutes and his commandments, which I am commanding you today for your own well-being and that of your descendants after you, so that you may long remain in the land that the Lord your God is giving you for all time.

DEUTERONOMY 4:27–40

What does my heart say?

- ° Where has the Lord scattered me in my life?
- ° Are there aspects of Church teaching about which I would like to know more? How can I find out?
- ° What does it mean to seek the Lord with all my heart and soul? What does that look like in practical terms?

~~~~~~

Rebellion

The Land of Make Believe only goes so far, even for an eight-year-old child. Susan's parents divorced when she was that age, and the impact was so forceful that she has no memory of what it was like when her family was together. After the divorce, Susan's two brothers went with her father, while she and her three sisters stayed with their mother. She cried herself to sleep at night; she loved both of her parents dearly and missed her father terribly. One of her sisters was sickly and another had an accident requiring hospitalization, taking a great deal of their mother's attention. Consequently, Susan was often left to herself, living in a fantasy world in which everything was okay and her family was back together again.

Her dreams were shattered when she turned eleven. Her father remarried, and when Susan turned thirteen, her mother remarried a man who had five children of his own. With nine kids and two adults sharing the same house, Susan struggled to find her place both spatially and emotionally. She began rebelling at age sixteen and distanced herself from the others.

During her senior year of high school, she met Ed and knew he was the right one for her. By the time she was twenty-one years old they had married, and within five-and-a-half years they had five children. At the urging of their parents, they had their children baptized in the Catholic Church and sent their two oldest children to Catholic grade school. Beyond that, there wasn't much Catholicism in the home. Mass attendance dropped completely away when Susan took on a full-time job. She and Ed worked opposite hours so that one of them would always be home with the kids.

The stress was too much, and Susan became bitter toward Ed.

They were anxious about providing for additional children, and she rebelled every time they couldn't afford something. Inevitably, they decided not to have any more children. Then things really started to fall apart. Susan began distancing herself from Ed. They had argued before, but it was different now. One day, she packed up the kids and went to her mom's house.

Being there reminded her of her grandparents who had recently passed away. Right up until they died, they ran a foster home for special needs children. Every night they would gather all of the kids, and anyone else who happened to be around, and pray the rosary together. Susan had always admired them, but she'd been away from the Church too long to imitate them. She couldn't pray on her own, so she pleaded with her grandparents for help. Ed incessantly called on the phone, begging her to come home. The memory of her grandparents made her realize nothing would be set right until she returned to the Church. She made this a condition for coming home, and Ed agreed.

Susan rearranged her work schedule so that the family could attend Mass together on Sundays. It was time for her oldest child to begin preparation for first reconciliation and first Communion. To help with the preparation, Susan and Ed were themselves being prepared for their reentry into the Church. Susan taught herself how to say the rosary and began saying it with the children every night. She received reconciliation for the first time in more than ten years. Ed remained skeptical but observant.

Some family friends invited them to attend a special Mass for the feast of the Assumption, during which the priest consecrated the entire parish to the Immaculate Heart of Mary. They went, not really sure what it was all about. They didn't understand the prayer, but they said it anyway. This seemingly insignificant event led to some very significant ones.

Susan cut back on her work hours, began home schooling, attended a Marian study group, and enrolled in *Catechism* classes. She and Ed's arguing abated somewhat, and he agreed to go with her to group meetings. They learned about the importance of the Holy Family as a model for all families and about God's divine providence. Susan began to see the error of her rebellious ways and the need to transform the roles of her family members to align more closely with those of the Holy Family. Their study group began preparation for Marian consecration, and within a year, they sealed their consecration with the Blessed Virgin Mary. Susan and Ed set up a prayer corner in their home dedicated to the Blessed Mother and had it blessed by a priest. It became the center of their home and family. They also began attending daily Mass and Eucharistic adoration. Things were starting to come together for them.

One issue remained unresolved. They were still closed to having more children, and this left Susan feeling unfulfilled with an aversion to intimacy. At the same time, she felt an increasing need to observe pious devotions and attend religious events; she even changed her style of dress. The more religious she became, the more Ed rebelled. She began searching for ways to compromise and to please and serve Ed more than in the past. She relied heavily on the Blessed Virgin Mary for strength and prayed fervently for guidance. As time went on, she could see the transformation in Ed. The relationship was changing for the better, and they started praying together. They felt ready for more children, and Susan was pregnant four months later. They had two more children within the next five years.

Looking back, Susan can see that rebellion was the root of her entire life's struggle, and yet God kept a hand on her the entire time. She thinks of Eve and of the two punishments God gave her: to be submissive to Adam and to have pain in childbearing. She's experienced these same two consequences firsthand but also has experienced abundant blessings through them.

What does Scripture say?

Therefore, as the Holy Spirit says, "Today, if you hear his voice, do not harden your hearts as in the rebellion, as on the day of testing in the wilderness, where your ancestors put me to the test, though they had seen my works for forty years. Therefore I was angry with that generation, and I said, 'They always go astray in their hearts, and they have not known my ways.' As in my anger I swore, 'They will not enter my rest.'" Take care, brothers and sisters, that none of you may have an evil, unbelieving heart that turns away from the living God. But exhort one another every day, as long as it is called "today," so that none of you may be hardened by the deceitfulness of sin. For we have become partners of Christ, if only we hold our first confidence firm to the end. As it is said, "Today, if you hear his voice, do not harden your hearts as in the rebellion."

HEBREWS 3:7–15

What does my heart say?

- ° Have I ever had a problem that I simply wanted to ignore? How did I handle it? What was the result?
- ° Am I a rebellious or a submissive person? What makes me that way?
- ° What do I know of the story of the Israelites? How is it similar or different from my own?

Scripture Manifestation

Bill had had about enough religion for one lifetime. His mother was a convert from Lutheranism, and his father was a baptized Catholic. They raised him as a Catholic, keeping the precepts of the Church and practicing the Catholic rituals and traditions like all good Catholic families in the 1960s.

Eventually, Bill became bored. Catholicism didn't offer anything new and exciting, and he felt as though he were being taught the same things over and over again. He went through the motions of receiving the sacrament of confirmation, but afterwards didn't feel as though there were any point in continuing. There was a lot of confusion in the post-Vatican II Church, and he wasn't interested enough to try to figure things out. At age twelve, Bill was done.

By the time he went to college, church and God were irrelevant to him. He was assigned a dormitory room with two "Bible Christians" in the room next to his, two more in the room next to them, and one in the room on the other side of Bill's. His dorm neighbors read their Bibles regularly and knew their Scripture well. Bill didn't. Even so, Bill considered them decent guys, and they all grew to be good friends. They hung out together, and inevitably the conversation gravitated toward religion. They questioned Bill about Catholic beliefs, and he tried to answer them, but he wasn't very convincing. He tried to go to Mass regularly, but that didn't work out. So he found a Bible and a Catholic *Catechism* and started reading.

One day a Jewish friend asked Bill to tell her about Jesus: He didn't know how. He saw a booklet published by Campus Crusade for Christ on faith sharing, and he read through it eagerly. The booklet outlined four principles pertaining to sin, God's love for us, and God's plan for our lives. The last principle really shook Bill. It mentioned that we all have a throne in our life, that which is our life center and authority. Unless Christ sits on that throne, our lives will be nothing but confusion and imbalance. Bill was incredulous and wondered why no one had ever told him that before. He was sure that this is what he was looking for. He prayed to Jesus, asking him to forgive his sins and come into his life. His favorite verse of the Bible became John 14:21: "They who have my commandments and keep them are those who love me; and those who love me will be loved by my Father, and I will love them and reveal myself to them." Bill wanted Jesus to manifest himself to him.

Then Bill became curious. If the Catholic Church hadn't told him about the need to make Jesus the center of his life, what else had it not told him? He could no longer consider himself a Catholic. His parents weren't very happy about his decision, and he reluctantly agreed to speak to a priest at their request. He was too prideful for it to do much good.

He joined a nondenominational Bible church and soon afterward married Joyce, a Presbyterian. Together they joined the Bible church. When their twin sons were born, they declined baptism because the church taught that infant baptism wasn't scriptural. Two years later, they moved to Joyce's hometown and joined the Presbyterian Church in which she'd been raised. Their daughter was born, and Bill became convinced that infant baptism was right after all, so they had all three of their children baptized.

Eight years later, Bill and Joyce joined a Bible study group directed by a reformed Episcopal minister. Bill started to notice some inconsistencies among the various Protestant churches. They couldn't agree on much of anything with one notable exception: They all agreed that the Catholic Church was wrong. Bill realized that all the Protestant churches he'd encountered claimed to believe what the Bible taught, but they all believed fundamentally different things. He could see that God speaks to us personally through the Bible but doesn't tell us all individually what to believe.

About that time, new neighbors moved in next door. They were a devout Catholic family, and Bill could tell that they were faith-filled and had a real relationship with Christ. They made such a big impression on Bill that he decided to go to Mass a couple of times, just to check it out. He was beginning to think that perhaps the Catholic Church wasn't so wrong after all, and yet he still had questions that he couldn't answer.

Still searching, Bill and his family joined the Lutheran Church Missouri Synod, where they stayed for several years. But Bill continued to have a feeling that something was missing. He started reading more about the Catholic Church and began bringing his family to Mass. Bill's parents were very supportive of course, and did their best to see that they made it to Mass for all the Holy Days of Obligation. One of those days was the feast of Mary Mother of God, and the homily had an earthshaking effect on Bill. It made him realize that it was time to do something about his indecision over the various denominations. It was time to go back to the Catholic Church.

That week, Bill went to a Catholic bookstore and loaded up on good Catholic reading. Eventually, Joyce read the books too, and before long she announced that she wanted to enter the RCIA program. Something stirred in Bill, and he received reconciliation for the first time in sixteen years. Joyce was received into the Church on the following Easter.

After more than a decade and a half of searching, Bill discovered what he had been missing. God nourishes life in us through both Word and sacrament, and these can only be found in the Catholic

Church. Additionally, faith hinges on authority, and the Catholic Church is the only church with authority that has been consistent since the time of Christ. For Bill, there's no other way. He simply can't get enough of the Catholic Church.

What does Scripture say?

And just then some people were carrying a paralyzed man lying on a bed. When Jesus saw their faith, he said to the paralytic, "Take heart, son; your sins are forgiven." Then some of the scribes said to themselves, "This man is blaspheming." But Jesus, perceiving their thoughts, said, "Why do you think evil in your hearts? For which is easier, to say, 'Your sins are forgiven,' or to say, 'Stand up and walk'? But so that you may know that the Son of Man has authority on earth to forgive sins"—he then said to the paralytic—"stand up, take your bed and go to your home." And he stood up and went to his home. When the crowds saw it, they were filled with awe, and they glorified God, who had given such authority to human beings.

MATTHEW 9:2–8

When he entered the temple, the chief priests and the elders of the people came to him as he was teaching, and said, "By what authority are you doing these things, and who gave you this authority?" Jesus said to them, "I will also ask you one question; if you tell me the answer, then I will also tell you by what authority I do these things. Did the baptism of John come from heaven, or was it of human origin?" And they argued with one another, "If we say, 'From heaven,' he will say to us, 'Why then did you not believe him?' But if we say, 'Of human origin,' we are afraid of the crowd; for all regard John as a prophet." So they answered Jesus, "We do not know." And he said to them, "Neither will I tell you by what authority I am doing these things.

MATTHEW 21:23–27

Then Jesus summoned his twelve disciples and gave them authority over unclean spirits, to cast them out, and to cure every disease and every sickness.

MATTHEW 10:1

Now the eleven disciples went to Galilee, to the mountain to which Jesus had directed them. When they saw him, they worshiped him; but some doubted. And Jesus came and said to them, "All authority in heaven and on earth has been given to me. Go therefore and make disciples of all nations, baptizing them in the name of the Father and of the Son and of the Holy Spirit, and teaching them to obey everything that I have commanded you. And remember, I am with you always, to the end of the age."

MATTHEW 28:16–20

What does my heart say?

- How do I define the term "authority?"
  What effect does authority have on me?
- What is a manifestation?
  How can Jesus manifest himself to me?
- Which of the Scripture passages included above
  speak the loudest to me? Why?

∿∿∿∿

Back on Track

Trisha knew that she'd somehow gotten off-track, but she continued full-steam ahead anyway. Born into a Catholic family with ten children, she practiced her Catholic faith until she married a non-Catholic man. Then she just drifted away from the Church. It was hard to keep being Catholic when her husband, Tad, wasn't. The situation was made worse when the rest of Trisha's family also fell away from the Church. She felt like she didn't have anybody to support her in her Catholicism.

She joined a Baptist church, and then a Methodist church. She felt like she was really getting to know Jesus and was quite happy. She had one sister who clung to her Catholic faith, and she would call Trisha from time to time, trying to convince her to come back to the Catholic Church. Trisha didn't want to hear any of it. She had her own thoughts on contraception and abortion, thoughts that didn't coincide with the teachings of the magisterium, and she wasn't about to let anyone change her mind. Whenever her sister called, she set the phone away from her ear and just let her talk. Whenever her sister promised that she would pray for Trisha and her family, Trisha sighed and rolled her eyes. She had no problems with the way she was living her life, why should her sister?

One day just before Easter, Trisha's sister decided to give it one more valiant effort. She called and asked Trisha, "Do you believe in sin?"

"No, not really," Trisha answered. "I mean, I do believe that we shouldn't kill, we shouldn't commit adultery, and we shouldn't steal. But beyond that, sin doesn't mean much to me. I don't do the big bad things, and I'm tired of the Church always telling me no, no, no, about everything. I'm a good person. That's all I need."

"You need to think about something," her sister said. "Sin isn't always the big things. Sin can be the little things that offend God. They seem trifling at the time, but bit by bit they build up until they become big things."

That night Trisha woke up in the middle of the night with her heart pounding. What her sister said about sin had gotten through to her. She knew she had offended God in many ways and felt sorry. She had been stubborn and insisted on control of her own life, of her own decisions, and of her own beliefs.

She told God, "I don't want to be in charge anymore. You be in charge!" She was beginning to have a new understanding of who Jesus was.

At about that time, her eight-year-old son became friends with a little boy down the street. The little boy and his family went to the Baptist church just around the corner from their house, and Trisha's son wanted to go with them. Trisha saw no harm in this, so she agreed. The two friends participated in various church activities, and Trisha would often drive them. Usually, she just dropped them off and left. But she kept thinking about the conversation she'd had with her sister about sin and decided that she'd better start going herself.

Strangely, Trisha enjoyed the services, but she found that she couldn't really pray there. So after the Baptist services, she would drive over to her old Catholic church, descend the stairs, and pray in front of the Pietà in the basement chapel. This continued for thirteen years.

A job transfer took Trisha and her family to another state, and she found a Methodist church she liked. One of Tad's coworkers was Catholic, and his wife wanted to open a Catholic bookstore. They asked Trisha for advice because they knew she had previously worked in a Christian bookstore. Trisha declined, saying she was too busy, and she wished them well. Then she lost her job, had difficulty finding a new one, and found herself with time on her hands. She offered to help with the Catholic bookstore.

During one of her shifts at the store, Trisha became bored and needed something to read, so she grabbed a book off the shelf. It happened to be Scott Hahn's Rome Sweet Home. She started reading it, and the more she read it, the more she was amazed. She had discovered the Truth. She went to her minister for consultation and confided to him, "I think I'm going to be a closet Catholic." She knew she had to go back to the Catholic Church.

Breaking her association with the Methodist Church wasn't easy. She was a Sunday school teacher there and deeply involved in other ministries of the church. The hardest part was attending the Methodist services, because she knew in her heart that she could no longer take their communion. She went back to her minister and told him she had to go. When she went to work the following Tuesday, she was a mess of emotion. As she walked into the store, she looked up at the store owner and burst into tears. The owner put her arms around Trisha and simply said, "Welcome back."

It's striking to Trisha that throughout the years she'd spontaneously prayed the same prayer every single day. "God, please don't let me go off-track. If I'm headed in the wrong direction, show me the right way." At the same time, she didn't know why she prayed that prayer, but now she does.

For the first time in twenty-six years, Trisha received the sacrament of reconciliation. That night, she heard that there would be a healing Mass at her new Catholic parish, and she went. During the Mass, she could feel the healing power of Jesus and knew she was back on the right track. And she's going full-steam ahead.

What does Scripture say?

One of the Pharisees asked Jesus to eat with him, and he went into the Pharisee's house and took his place at the table. And a woman in the city, who was a sinner, having learned that he was eating in the Pharisee's house, brought an alabaster jar of ointment. She stood behind him at his feet, weeping, and began to bathe his feet with her tears and to dry them with her hair. Then she continued kissing his feet and anointing them with the ointment. Now when the Pharisee who had invited him saw it, he said to himself, "If this man were a prophet, he would have known who and what kind of woman this is who is touching him—that she is a sinner." Jesus spoke up and said to him, "Simon, I have something to say to you." "Teacher," he replied, "Speak." "A certain creditor had two debtors; one owed five hundred *denarii*, and the other fifty. When they could not pay, he canceled the debts for both of them. Now which of them will love him more?" Simon answered, "I suppose the one for whom he canceled the greater debt." And Jesus said to him, "You have judged rightly." Then turning toward the woman, he said to Simon, "Do you see this woman? I entered your house; you gave me no water for my feet, but she has bathed my feet with her tears and dried them with her hair. You gave me no kiss, but from the time I came in she has not stopped kissing my feet. You did not anoint my head with oil, but she has anointed my feet with ointment. Therefore, I tell you, her sins, which were many, have been forgiven; hence she has shown great love. But the one to whom little is forgiven, loves little." Then he said to her, "Your sins are forgiven." But those who were at the table with him began to say among themselves, "Who is this who even forgives sins?" And he said to the woman, "Your faith has saved you; go in peace."

LUKE 7:36–50

What does my heart say?

- How do I know when I'm on or off the right track? At work? At home? In my relationships?
- Is there someone in my life to whom I don't want to listen? Who is it? Why don't I want to listen?
- What does Jesus mean by
  "But the one to whom little is forgiven, loves little"?

Change of Heart

Laziness. That's the way Heather describes it. She had no real reason for leaving the Catholic Church, other than the fact that when she started college she stopped going to church because no one else did. Like most of her peers, she felt it was inconvenient to get up early on Sunday mornings. She had other things to do like sleeping in, going to parties, boyfriends, work, and other distractions. At that time in her life, all she was interested in was finding the right guy to marry.

She found Kyle, and they got engaged. She thought she had everything she ever wanted and needed. But in the months leading up to the wedding, she discovered some disturbing things about her fiancé. She'd always known that he was a non-practicing Catholic, but some moral issues surfaced that kept her up at night. She started dreading everything wedding-related and became filled with fear and despair.

She couldn't believe this was happening to her, the person who had always and only wanted to be married. She couldn't explain it, but she knew God could.

She started talking to God and even began going to Mass again. She figured since they were planning a Catholic wedding, this would be the thing to do. She started talking to a priest about the situation, and somewhere between going back to Mass, praying, and consulting with the priest, it became clear that she and Kyle should not get married.

She embarked on a private prayer crusade, begging God to change Kyle's heart so they could make things work. God didn't change Kyle's heart, but he did something even better. He gave Heather the strength to end the engagement just two weeks before the wedding. It was one of the hardest things she'd ever done in her life, but she knew ending the relationship two weeks before the wedding was so much better than ending it two weeks after.

After she finally ended it, she became wracked with guilt, fear, sadness, and loneliness. Her heart was in absolute turmoil. She was in so much emotional pain that she could barely stand it. In spite of her anguish, she felt God's voice deep in her heart. It said, "Now, I want you back with me." She gladly went. In the past, she'd been faced with a choice between two men, and it had been extremely difficult. Now she was faced with a choice between God and man, and she found it to be an easy one. The ending of the relationship with her fiancé was painful, but she was sustained by God's grace and came through the ordeal with far less trauma than she would ever have imagined. Because she had given herself up to God, she could feel herself resting in God's arms, and she felt secure there.

Heather lives in gratitude, aware now that God has always been calling her even when she has refused to listen. Her broken engagement was the means God used to pull her out of her laziness and enable her to open her ears and heart to God, just in time.

What does Scripture say?

There is severe discipline for one who forsakes the way, but one who hates a rebuke will die. Sheol and Abaddon lie open before the LORD, how much more human hearts! Scoffers do not like to be rebuked; they will not go to the wise. A glad heart makes a cheerful countenance, but by sorrow of heart the spirit is broken. The mind of one who has understanding seeks knowledge, but the mouths of fools feed on folly. All the days of the poor are hard, but a cheerful heart has a continual feast. Better is a little with the fear of the LORD than great treasure and trouble with it. Better is a dinner of vegetables where love is than a fatted ox and hatred with it. Those who are hot-tempered stir up strife, but those who are slow to anger calm contention. The way of the lazy is overgrown with thorns, but the path of the upright is a level highway. A wise child makes a glad father, but the foolish despise their mothers. Folly is a joy to one who has no sense, but a person of understanding walks straight ahead. Without counsel, plans go wrong, but with many advisers they succeed. To make an apt answer is a joy to anyone, and a word in season, how good it is!

PROVERBS 15:10–23

What does my heart say?

- ° Do I ever let laziness get in the way of accomplishing things? What are those things? Why do I feel too lazy to do them?
- ° Do I seek counsel when I have a difficult decision to make? To whom do I go? How do I know when it's time to seek counsel?
- ° How does the Scripture passage above touch me?

〰〰〰

Anxious and Misinformed

Arlene had been diagnosed with a brain tumor. A craniotomy was scheduled, but at sixty-nine years of age there were some added risks involved. It wouldn't be an easy surgery; there were no sure bets. Arlene was certain she was going to die. At best, she figured that if she did survive she would be changed forever. One false move by the surgeon, and she could end up disabled for the rest of her life. The uncertainty and anxiety were overwhelming, and Arlene was scared.

Her doctor was concerned about Arlene's anxiety and recommended that she seek treatment from a psychologist. Sadly, it didn't help much. She was just as anxious as before, if not more so.

One Saturday afternoon before the surgery, she lay down to rest. She was trying not to think about the risks and consequences of surgery and hoping that she could calm down enough to sleep. Suddenly, she was overcome by an irrepressible feeling that she had to go to confession. It had been forty years since she had last received reconciliation. A number of unpleasant experiences and disagreements with church teaching, especially in regard to contraception, had caused her to lapse from her Catholic faith, and she just stayed away.

She doesn't remember the drive to the church, but she does

remember her confession. When she got there, the young assistant pastor's door was open and she thought to herself, "He's the tough one. I deserve to be chastised." So she went in. They discussed her life and her reservations, not with God, but with the hierarchy of the Church. As a young mother, she'd had four children in five years and was struggling both financially and emotionally. A priest told her that she had to have as many children as God sent her no matter what, and could by no means prevent a pregnancy.

The assistant pastor listened to her story and gently explained that the Church does allow for natural family planning during difficult circumstances, and that Arlene had been misinformed. He apologized for some of the "hardness" she had encountered and listened very carefully to her sins. At the end of the conversation, he instructed Arlene to go into the chapel where the Eucharist was and offer her surgery to Jesus. She did, and miraculously she experienced a sense of peace. It was truly in God's hands now, and the anxiety left her.

Since Arlene couldn't remember the act of contrition, the priest had recommended that she make up her own. She did, and she further promised God that she would serve God in some way if she survived. The surgery was on a Tuesday. Arlene left the hospital on Friday and was at Mass the following Sunday. She's a new woman physically, mentally, and spiritually and ready to serve the Lord in whatever way God chooses. She's given her life to God, and she doesn't want it back.

What does Scripture say?

Humble yourselves therefore under the mighty hand of God, so that he may exalt you in due time. Cast all your anxiety on him, because he cares for you.

Discipline yourselves, keep alert. Like a roaring lion your adversary the devil prowls around, looking for someone to devour. Resist him, steadfast in your faith, for you know that your brothers and sisters in all the world are undergoing the same kinds of suffering.

And after you have suffered for a little while, the God of all grace, who has called you to his eternal glory in Christ, will himself restore, support, strengthen, and establish you. To him be the power forever and ever. Amen.

1 PETER 5:6–11

What does my heart say?

- ° Are there things in my life about which I'm anxious? What are they? Why am I anxious about them?
- ° Are there teachings of the Church with which I disagree? Is it possible that I've been misinformed about them? Is it possible that I've been under-catechized and therefore don't understand them?
- ° Saint Peter urges us to discipline ourselves and keep alert. How can I do that?

Conclusion

The doors slid open, and I stepped onto the platform. I'd seen Grand Central Station in the movies but never in person. A naïve nineteen-year-old from the Midwest, I felt lost, overwhelmed, and scared out of my wits. I didn't know the first thing about fending for myself in a big city. I dragged my trailer-sized suitcase out to the street and hailed a taxi. Half an hour later, we pulled up in front of the Manhattan skyscraper where my sister worked. I paid the driver, got out, and walked around to the back of the taxi. The driver came around and opened the trunk. He grabbed my suitcase and flung it onto the sidewalk with such force that it burst open, the contents spewing all over the concrete. The taxi driver pulled away while I tried to gather my belongings before they were trampled into uselessness. That was what happened to people who neglected to tip taxi drivers, even if it was for lack of metropolitan savvy.

My sister, a rising executive in a prestigious firm, had invited me to visit her in New York. I'd recently become engaged, and she thought it would be a great opportunity for me to learn some of the ways of the world before I was married. She also thought it would be an opportunity to dissuade me from what she perceived as my ridiculous Catholic notions and rigid adherence to Church teachings. I agreed to go, thinking it would be a great opportunity to dissuade her from what I perceived to be her progressive views and disregard for Church authority. It didn't work for either of us.

We started out having lots of fun. She showed me around her office and introduced me to some of her coworkers. We saw some of the sights and went shopping together. We hung out and ate at a Chinese restaurant. That was our mistake.

It wasn't the food that led to our demise; it was the topic of conversation. Unable to keep up the charade any longer, we decided it was time to straighten each other out. It was time to talk about Catholicism.

We began politely enough, but quickly dropped the small talk and dug into the heart of the matter—or should I say jugular of the matter. Sharing the same explosive and stubborn temperament, we were bound to be at each other's throats before long. And we were. The discussion turned to an argument, our tempers escalated, and our voices rose. I was so frustrated, I picked up my fork and banged it on the tabletop, as if that would do any good in helping me make my point. The next moment, the restaurant manager appeared. He stood next to our table, hands gently clasped in front of him, and cleared his throat. His posture was meek, but his eyes strongly recommended that we take it outside. So we did.

Sadly, it's still outside. Our rage and obstinacy served only to make each of us even more set in our ways, causing a lasting aversion to talking about anything having to do with faith or morals. I'd let my temper get the best of me and instead of drawing her closer, I'd pushed her away. We'll always love each other, but now there's an underlying strain that might not have been there if I'd approached the situation with charity, not chagrin.

I'd like to think that I've matured over the years. I've still got my hot temper, and my ire is still apt to rise quickly, but I keep it in better check. At least I hope so. I realize now that it does no good to bicker or force a point. That only makes the other person defensive and even less likely to listen.

The Crusades had their place in time, but for me today the best tactic is to proceed without sword and shield. I've adopted the philosophy of "show, don't tell." That doesn't mean that I'll let others walk all over the Catholic faith—misconceptions and fallacies must be corrected, and we're always required to speak the Truth—but I'll approach with benevolence, not belittlement. The greatest "weapon" I have is the testimony of a life lived in joy, humility, and Christian values. It will be the impression I leave—not the words I fling—that will bring others back to the Catholic Church.